The Needlework of
MARY
Queen of Scots

The Needlework of
MARY
Queen of Scots

Margaret Swain

RUTH BEAN

First published (hardbound) 1973 by Van Nostrand Reinhold Co. Inc.

This edition published in 1986 in Great Britain by
Ruth Bean Publishers, an imprint of The Crowood Press
Ramsbury, Marlborough, Wiltshire, SN8 2HR

www.crowood.com

This impression 2013

ISBN 978 0 903585 22 4

Printed in China

Contents

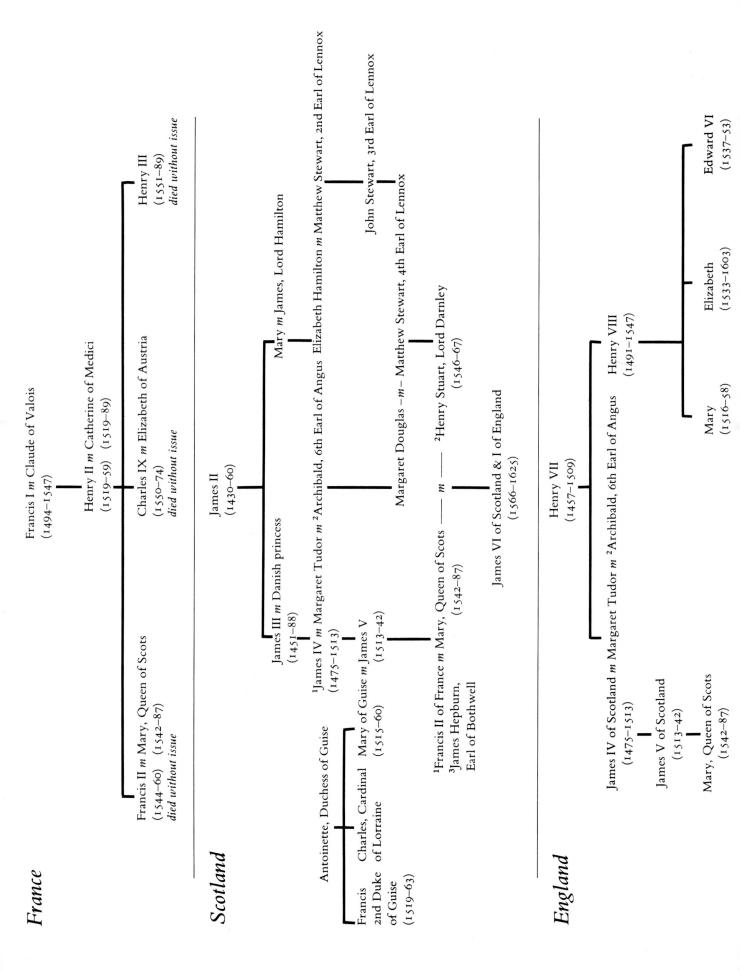

France

Francis I *m* Claude of Valois
(1494–1547)

Henry II *m* Catherine of Medici
(1519–59)   (1519–89)

Charles IX *m* Elizabeth of Austria
(1550–74)
died without issue

Henry III
(1551–89)
died without issue

Francis II *m* Mary, Queen of Scots
(1544–60)   (1542–87)
died without issue

Scotland

James II
(1430–60)

James III *m* Danish princess
(1451–88)

Mary *m* James, Lord Hamilton   Elizabeth Hamilton *m* Matthew Stewart, 2nd Earl of Lennox

[1]James IV *m* Margaret Tudor *m* [2]Archibald, 6th Earl of Angus   John Stewart, 3rd Earl of Lennox
(1475–1513)

Mary of Guise *m* James V
(1515–60)   (1513–42)

Antoinette, Duchess of Guise

Francis   Charles, Cardinal   Mary of Guise
2nd Duke   of Lorraine   (1515–60)
of Guise
(1519–63)

[1]Francis II of France *m* Mary, Queen of Scots ——— *m* ——— [2]Henry Stuart, Lord Darnley
(1542–87)   (1546–67)
[3]James Hepburn,   Margaret Douglas –*m*– Matthew Stewart, 4th Earl of Lennox
Earl of Bothwell

James VI of Scotland & I of England
(1566–1625)

England

Henry VII
(1457–1509)

James IV of Scotland *m* Margaret Tudor *m* [2]Archibald, 6th Earl of Angus   Henry VIII
(1475–1513)   (1491–1547)

James V of Scotland
(1513–42)

Mary, Queen of Scots
(1542–87)

Mary   Elizabeth   Edward VI
(1516–58)   (1533–1603)   (1537–53)

Calendar

1542	*8 December*	Birth of Mary Stuart, daughter of James V of Scotland and Marie de Guise.
	14 December	Death of James V. Mary succeeded to the throne of Scotland.
1543	*9 September*	Coronation of the infant Queen of Scots.
1548	*7 August*	Mary sent to France to be brought up with the children of the French King, Henry II.
1558	*24 April*	Marriage of Mary and Francis, Dauphin of France.
	17 November	Elizabeth succeeded to the throne of England.
1559	*10 July*	Death of Henry II. The Dauphin became Francis II of France and Mary became Queen of France.
1560	*11 June*	Death of Marie de Guise, Regent of Scotland.
	11 August	The Scottish parliament established the reformed Protestant religion in Scotland.
	5 December	Death of Francis II, succeeded by his young brother Charles IX.
1561	*19 August*	Mary returned to Scotland.
1562	*August – September*	Mary visited Inverness and Aberdeen. Rebellion of the Earl of Huntly and his son.
1565	*29 July*	Mary married Henry, Lord Darnley as her second husband.
1566	*9 March*	Murder of Mary's secretary, David Rizzio.
	19 June	Birth of Mary's son, James, later James VI of Scotland and I of England.
1567	*10 February*	Murder of Darnley.
	15 May	Mary married James Hepburn, Earl of Bothwell as her third husband.
	15 June	Battle of Carberry Hill. Mary taken prisoner by her nobles. Bothwell outlawed and escaped to Denmark, where he later died in prison.
	16 June	Mary imprisoned in the island of Lochleven.
	29 July	The infant James crowned King of Scots, after Mary had signed an instrument of abdication. James Stewart, Earl of Moray became Regent.
1568	*2 May*	Mary escaped from Lochleven.
	May	Mary's supporters were defeated at the battle of Langside.
	16 May	Mary fled to England, landing at Workington, Cumberland.
	18 May	Mary lodged in Carlisle Castle, afterwards moved to Bolton Castle, Yorkshire.
1569	*January*	The Earl of Shrewsbury became the custodian of Mary, first at Tutbury Castle, then at Sheffield.
1570		Secret marriage plans between Mary and the Duke of Norfolk.
1572		Execution of the Duke of Norfolk for his part in the plot against Queen Elizabeth.
1584		Mary taken from the charge of the Earl of Shrewsbury.
1585	*January*	Imprisoned at Tutbury under Sir Amyas Paulet.
	Autumn	Moved to Chartley Hall, Staffordshire.
1586		The Babington Plot.
	September	Mary taken to Fotheringhay Castle.
	15 October	Trial of Mary Queen of Scots.
1587	*8 February*	Execution of Mary at Fotheringhay.

AUTHOR'S NOTE

THE NEEDLEWORK of Mary Stuart has never been completely illustrated since the hangings at Oxburgh Hall were first described by Francis de Zulueta in the illuminating monograph published in 1923, and now out of print. In this book all the known pieces which bear her cipher or monogram are reproduced, as well as others attributed to her.

MY THANKS are especially due to Mr. Donald King, Keeper, and to Miss Santina Levey, Research Assistant, of the Department of Textiles, the Victoria and Albert Museum, who kindly arranged for the photography of the panels of the Oxburgh hangings, some of them specially for this book. I must also thank Mr. John Nevinson for the generous loan of his notes on the Oxburgh and Hardwick embroideries, Lady Bedingfeld and Mrs. Hartcup, who received me so hospitably at Oxburgh Hall, and Mr. R. E. Hutchison, Keeper, the Scottish National Portrait Gallery, for his advice on the choice of portraits. I am deeply grateful to Mrs. A. M. Leach for the lacis and blackwork diagrams, to Mrs. Dorothy Sim for the loan of her thesis *Mary, Queen of Scots, her surviving needlework*, and for the charts of Mary's cipher and the Hardwick design, and to Barrie & Jenkins for the use of the stitch diagrams from my book *Historical Needlework*.

I have received welcome help and advice from many, especially the Very Rev. J. Brennan, Rector of Blairs College, Aberdeen, Miss Pamela Clabburn, of Strangers Hall Museum, Norwich, Mr. C. P. Finlayson, the Department of Manuscripts, the University Library, Edinburgh, Dr. Georg Garde, Copenhagen, Mr. Stuart Maxwell, the National Museum of Scottish Antiquities, Mr. Revel Oddy, the Royal Scottish Museum, and Mr. Francis W. Steer, Librarian to His Grace the Duke of Norfolk. To all these, and to the owners who so courteously allowed their embroideries to be used as illustrations, my thanks are offered, and to my husband, who, as always, encouraged and supported me in the writing of this book.

List of plates

Bold type indicates colour

MARIA
D G
SCOTIÆ
PIISSIMA REGINA
FRANCIÆ DOTARIA
ANNO
ÆTATIS REGNIQ
36
ANGLICÆ CAPTIVIT
10
S H
1578

FRONTISPIECE
The Sheffield Portrait of Mary, Queen of Scots, said to be painted by P. Oudry.

FRANCE

1 Childhood

She became Queen when she was only six days old. Her father, James V of Scotland, died suddenly (some say mysteriously) on December 14th, 1542, at the age of thirty, leaving as his only legitimate heir the baby girl. Mary was the third child born to James and Marie de Guise, James's second wife. Two sons had died in infancy, and the birth of a female child, followed so rapidly by the death of the King, was regarded as a great disaster in Scotland. In the words of John Knox 'all men lamented that the realm was left without a male to succeed'.

Mary's father had himself succeeded to the throne as an infant after his father James IV had been killed fighting against England at the battle of Flodden in 1513, and the kingdom had been torn then by the perpetual feuds of the most powerful families of Scotland, most of them related to the royal house of Stewart. The young king's widowed mother, Margaret Tudor, had subsequently married one of the Scottish nobles, Archibald, Earl of Angus, who became Regent during the childhood of the King, and his extravagance and greed had caused bitter envy and strife. Now another infant – this time a girl – succeeded, with the inevitable power-struggle for the regency, while England was poised to invade and seize the country after the defeat of the Scottish army at the battle of Solway Moss – a defeat that some said had broken the heart of Mary's father and caused his death.

Scotland and England were still two separate and independent kingdoms, although Henry VIII, King of England, the brother of Queen Margaret, regarded himself as overlord of the smaller realm of Scotland. Following the death of James V and the birth of a female successor, Henry proposed by the Treaty of Greenwich an end to the centuries-long warfare between Scotland and England. Henry had a son, the future Edward VI, then aged six, and it was suggested that the infant Queen of Scots should be brought up at the English court and become Edward's bride, thus uniting the two kingdoms by marriage. The Scottish nobles, especially those receiving a subsidy from the English King, agreed, but the treaty was never put into effect.

Instead, the regency struggle continued all through the summer of 1542. The Protestant, pro-English party were overruled by a Catholic regency subsidised by French money. Mary was crowned at Stirling at the age of nine months, and Henry VIII resumed the warfare. He devastated the south of Scotland, and defeated yet another Scottish army at the battle of Pinkie Cleugh, a few miles from Edinburgh, in 1547.

It was this defeat that finally persuaded the Scots that any hope of withstanding the English lay in obtaining help from France. The French King, Henry II, agreed to send military assistance in January, 1548. In return the young Queen was to be sent to France and brought up at the French court as the future bride of his eldest son, the Dauphin Francis. The Queen's mother, Marie de Guise, agreed readily. As the betrothed of Edward Tudor Mary would have been brought up a Protestant. As the bride of the future French King, Mary would be brought up a Catholic, under the care of her grandmother, the Duchess Antoinette de Guise, and of her uncles, the Duke de Guise and his brother, the Cardinal of Lorraine. But the final parting with her small daughter was painful. On August 7th, 1548, Mary sailed from Scotland with her ladies, her gentlemen and her four Maries, the young girls of noble family, in galleys sent by the King of France. She landed in France after a stormy voyage six days later.

The French court at which she arrived had become under Francis I the most brilliant in Europe. His son, Henry II, who had sent the galleys for Mary, was as cultivated as his father, but lacked his gaiety and exuberance. He had inherited his father's passion for hunting, and had a genuine affection for his children.

Henry's wife, Catherine de Medici, had been orphaned at birth. She had been starved of affection as a child in Florence, where, as heiress of the Medicis, she had been regarded merely as a bargaining pawn. The only happy period of her singularly loveless childhood had been spent in a Florentine convent, where she had been placed for safety. Her marriage to Henry had been equally loveless. The uncrowned queen of the court was the legendary Diane de Poitiers, who had become the king's mistress in her widowhood, even though twenty years older than the young prince. He remained devoted to her till the day of his death, by which time she was nearly sixty. She shared the King's passion for hunting. Indeed her unfading beauty and superb health may have owed more to her habit of rising early to ride, than to the asses' milk baths she is reputed to have enjoyed.

Queen Catherine accepted Henry's devotion to Diane with dignity and hid her feelings. She had the additional anguish of having had to wait ten years for the birth of her first child. She then bore nine more delicate, highly strung children in rapid succession. When Mary arrived to share the royal nursery, the Dauphin Francis was four. Elizabeth, later to be the third wife of Philip II of Spain, was three, and Claude was a baby girl of just over a year. After Mary's arrival there followed Charles (later Charles IX), born in 1550; Henry (III) in 1551; Francis, Duke of Alençon, in 1554; and the following year Marguerite (la Reine Margot who married Henry of Navarre). Catherine's three other children died in infancy.

Perhaps because she had had to wait so long to become a mother Catherine was almost over-solicitous about her children's health and welfare. The royal nursery was also supervised by Diane de Poitiers to an extent that seems surprising today. Diane it was who suggested changes in the nursery regime to the King, and even trained the royal nursemaids before they were appointed by Catherine. The position of king's mistress was regarded with a more tolerant eye than it would be today. Certainly the upbringing of Diane's own two daughters – one the child of her dead husband, the other the king's child – was firmly conventional. Diane's concern for and interest in all the royal children's illnesses and education appeared natural and genuine, and this even extended to the little Queen of Scots.

Mary's welfare was also closely supervised by her grandmother and her mother's brothers, the Duke de Guise and the Cardinal of Lorraine, both figures of immense influence and power. They did not underestimate the importance of being able to control the education of their niece, who, as crowned monarch of an independent kingdom, was a very desirable match for the future King of France. She was taught to believe that her future lay in France as the bride of the Dauphin. Indeed the idea of training her to rule Scotland appeared a relatively trivial matter, and the possibility of her returning to her native land seems not to have been considered.

In spite of all this, Mary's childhood at the French court seems to have been a very happy one. She shared a room at first with Elizabeth, the eldest Princess. Her four Maries, the young maids of honour who accompanied her – Mary Seton, Mary Fleming, Mary Beaton and Mary Livingstone – were sent off to a Dominican convent school, no doubt to encourage the little Queen to converse in French rather than in her own Scots tongue, which was considered uncouth by the French.

Mary was an intelligent, attractive child, and did her best to please these influential grown-ups. The King responded to her charm, calling her the most perfect child, and ordained that, as a crowned Queen and the future wife of the Dauphin, she should take precedence over his daughters. She listened attentively to all that her uncles taught her, and began to write dutiful letters to her mother, signed 'your humble and obedient daughter, Marie', echoing their instructions. She also asked her mother to write to the Duchess de Valentinois (the title bestowed on Diane de Poitiers by the King) to thank her for her kindness to her little daughter. If she pertly referred to Catherine de Medici within her hearing as 'a daughter of tradesmen', she was doubtless merely echoing what she had heard around her. Catherine ignored this as she had ignored all the other slights she had received.

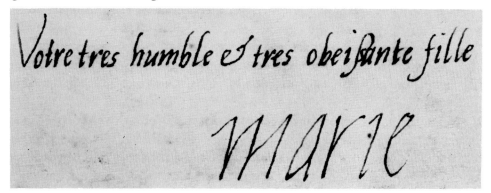

Plate 1
Signature of Mary when a young girl on a letter sent to her mother, Mary de Guise. All her life the Queen of Scots signed herself MARIE. (National Library of Scotland, Edinburgh.)

The royal children had their own establishment with ladies and gentlemen, chaplains, nurses and servants, as well as cooks, laundresses and stablemen. The size of this household rose steadily with each new baby. Because sanitation was so primitive, it was periodically necessary to move the whole household from one castle to another so that adequate cleansing could be carried out. For a move on such a scale horses, food and fodder had to be commandeered at the villages en route. For the royal children, however, the progress from one establishment to the next was surely a delightful interlude. They took their dogs – Mary had terriers, 'earth dogs', sent from Scotland – as well as their birds, falcons and hawks, and their horses. Riding was a necessity: it was the quickest and sometimes the only way of getting from one place to another, in an age in which the only other transport was heavy carriages with cumbersome wheels lurching over unmade often rocky roads. Mary became a fearless rider. She delighted in the exercise, and pined for it when she was kept from the saddle.

She learned to speak fluent French. She also learned Italian, the language of Catherine de Medici, and Latin, the language of the Catholic church and the civilised West, as well as Spanish and a little Greek. She was tall with an attractive voice, red-gold hair and beautiful hands. She learned to sing, to dance, to play the lute, to sew and embroider. She wore the rich clothes that befitted her rank in a court where clothing was sumptuous. When she was nine, material was bought – crimson and violet velvet, crimson silk damask from Venice, red taffeta and black taffeta lined with white or yellow or green taffeta – to be made into dresses. These were worn with separate sleeves, fronts and head-dresses of white, blue or crimson satin. In addition her tailor, Nicolas de Moncel, made for her a dress of gold damask banded with crimson satin, the sleeves slit and stiffened with buckram. Another dress was of cloth of silver with a hem of green satin, edged with silver lace and lined with white taffeta. A pair of sleeves and a front of white satin were sewn with a hundred and twenty diamonds and rubies. A coif and sleeves of violet velvet were adorned with gold buttons enamelled in black and white, the colours of Diane de Poitiers, and decorated with her sign, the crescent moon, symbol of the goddess Diana.

Mary's shifts and handkerchiefs were of the finest linen. She had a crystal mirror framed in velvet and adorned with ribbon bows. At meals she sat on a special chair, covered with green velvet, and was attended by two pages whose cloaks were banded with yellow velvet and edged with yellow and red braid. She had her own silver communion vessels, which were kept in a special box – perhaps to avoid infection but more likely as a precaution against poison.

So much grandeur and stiffness may appear suffocating to modern minds. To the little Queen of Scots, however, they were merely the marks of her rank, and she accepted them gladly. Like Elizabeth of England, she learned from her earliest years the peculiar disadvantages from which a female monarch suffered. As a Queen she had to use every art, including costume, to enhance her dignity and set herself apart.

In spite of her rank Mary was anything but lonely. It is true that she was separated from her mother, whom she loved and admired. Unlike Elizabeth of England, whose mother had been executed and who was brought up largely by her household of ladies and gentlemen, Mary was surrounded with affectionate admiration. She had a loving and devoted mother, who, although separated from her by the duty of governing her daughter's kingdom, took a passionate interest in every detail of her life and upbringing. Her grandmother, the Duchess Antoinette de Guise, her uncles and aunts, the King and Queen of France, all were committed to her welfare. The children, especially the Dauphin Francis, her intended husband and two years her junior, looked up to her as the eldest of the royal nursery.

It is not surprising that he should have been genuinely fond of her, with her charm and energy, her height, good looks and gentle gaiety. He himself was undersized and delicate, but his nervous energy forced him to compensate for this by undertaking physical exertions far beyond his feeble strength – greatly to the alarm of his mother. He hunted and learned archery and forms of combat in an attempt to overcome his puny physique.

The whole court watched the flowering of their romance. It was a tender affection based on childhood friendship. The Dauphin delighted in being with Mary. They rode and played cards together. She responded with the affection of an older, stronger, taller child towards a younger, weaker and more dependent one. In an age which utterly ignored the feelings of the bride in a royal marriage Mary was especially fortunate.

When she was nine, her mother arrived on a long-awaited visit to the French court, to the great joy of her little daughter. She was received with honour by Henry and Catherine, although she wearied them in the end by her constant pleas for money for Scotland. Her Guise relatives advised and exhorted her, and when she returned to the anxieties and austerities of life in Scotland at the end of twelve months, never to see her daughter again, it was demonstrated to Mary that her life and her future lay in France.

2 The Queen – Dauphiness

Mary lived in the age of the Reformation, at a time in which political and religious conflicts were inextricably mixed. In England the Protestantism started by Luther had been accepted by Henry VIII, and although England briefly reverted to Catholicism during the reign of Mary (1553–58), Henry's second daughter, Elizabeth, re-established the Protestant beliefs on her accession. In France the Calvinists or Huguenots, as the French Protestants were known, were regarded by Henry II and the Cardinal of Lorraine, Mary's uncle, as the enemies of the State. They were finally crushed, after the death of Henry, in the Massacre of St. Bartholomew's Eve, 1572. In Scotland, under the fervent promptings of John Knox, the teachings of Calvin were gaining ground. Indeed Calvinism was to become the official religion of Scotland adopted by the Scottish Parliament. Mary, brought up a Catholic at a Catholic court, wrote a *Letter to Calvin* as an exercise. He was at the time living and writing in Geneva, but it is unlikely that it was ever sent to him.

These rumblings of bitter religious strife do not appear to have disturbed the carefree life of the royal children who, between lessons and castles, had their dogs and ponies and birds, their music and games and dancing.

As Mary grew older, she began to take part in the ceremonies and pageants of what was one of the gayest and most brilliant of renaissance courts. Music and dancing, hunting and tournaments were arranged, and when active exercise was impossible, while Catherine sat watchfully embroidering in silks every afternoon, Mary and the young Princesses made music, wrote poems or read.

There were theological works and the poems of Pierre de Ronsard and Joachim du Bellay, both courtiers. Greek and Latin authors were studied in the schoolroom and translated. The royal children were children of the Renaissance, a time in which, as well as the ancient world, the curiosities of the New World were being written about, drawn and discussed. Brazil had been discovered by a Frenchman, and Jacques Cartier was still living, a respected figure in his home town of St. Malo, although his discovery of Canada and the St. Lawrence was regarded as unimportant because he had brought back neither diamonds nor gold.

Books on natural history were being published, founded on observation rather than on the myths of the Middle Ages. A Swiss physician, Conrad Gesner, published in 1551 the first of four folios on fishes, birds and mammals, clearly illustrated with woodcuts, giving them a new scientific classification.

Another physician, a Frenchman called Pierre Belon, an almost exact contemporary of Gesner and a keen naturalist with the same burning desire to examine and record, published in the same year a learned treatise on the dolphin, which he had dissected, distinguishing it from the porpoise, with which it had often been confused. He followed this in 1555 with a small, more popular books on fishes, *La Nature et Diversité des Poissons*, published in Paris, and an elegant folio on birds somewhat similar to that of Gesner, but in French, not the Latin of Gesner. All of these must have been familiar to Mary, for she used the woodcuts later for some of her embroidery designs.

There were also the entertaining new emblem books, which had come from Italy and were now being printed in France. These were picture books, each page showing an incident or surrealist situation with a Latin motto, often with a double meaning. In those times a pictorial emblem was often adopted by a royal or noble personage as a personal symbol, just as today advertisers try to find an easily recognisable symbol for a widely marketed product. Thus the symbol (or *impresa*) of Mary's mother, Marie de Guise, was the mythical bird the phoenix, which rises anew from the flames which have destroyed it. The motto was '*En Ma Fin Git Ma Commencement*' ('In my end lies my beginning'), for her two marriages had both ended in widowhood, yet out of the ashes of both sorrows she had made a new life. After her first husband died, she married the King of Scots, and after his death she became ruler of Scotland on her daughter's behalf.

Henry II of France took as his *impresa* three crescent moons, symbol of the goddess Diana (and of Diane de Poitiers) with the Latin motto '*Donec Totem Impleat Orbem*' ('Till he fills the whole world'), a motto that could be taken as referring to the light of the waxing moon or to the splendour of the King. This *impresa* was recognised as the king's personal emblem, so that, when he entered Paris after his accession, the Gate of St. Denis was decorated with two colossi bearing this symbol and motto.

The recognition and solving of emblems was as absorbing to the educated men and women of the period as crossword puzzles are today. In French, as well as in English, the spoken and written word was becoming more vivid and flexible, so that riddles, puns and anagrams, especially those translated from the universal Latin, had a freshness and meaning that today we can scarcely appreciate. Marguerite, the sister of Francis, took as her emblem the marigold which turns its face always to the sun, with the Latin motto '*Non Inferiora Secutus*' ('Not following lower things'). Although the flower in the emblem is the yellow marigold whose face turns to follow the sun, the shape in a woodcut is that of the marguerite or daisy, a play on the name of Marguerite. Mary took this emblem later, giving it a French motto '*Sa Virtu m'Atire*' ('Its strength draws me') which formed an anagram on her name MARIE STVART.

When Mary was sixteen, Henry decided that the long-awaited marriage should take place, and on Sunday April 24th, 1558, Mary and Francis were married with great magnificence at Notre Dame in Paris. It was the first time for many centuries that a Dauphin had been married in France, as the wedding usually took place in the country of the bride. Marriage to a crowned Queen added to the splendour, but it was the beauty and elegance of the young

Non inferiora sequutus.

Plate 2
Emblem. The Marigold turning to the sun, with the motto *'Non Inferiora Secutus'* ('Not following lower things'). The symbol or *impresa* of Marguerite of Navarre, it was taken by Mary as her own with the motto *'Sa Virtu m'Atire'* ('Its strength draws me') an anagram on her name MARIE STVART. From Paradin *Devises Heroiques*, Lyon, first published 1557. (National Library of Scotland, Edinburgh.)

bride, wearing shimmering white and blazing with diamonds, that captured the hearts of those who wrote about it.

The Commissioners from Scotland who signed the marriage treaty granted the title of King of Scotland to the Dauphin, so that Mary became Queen-Dauphiness. The Dauphin was now a sickly, undersized fifteen, but with Henry II in the prime of life there appeared plenty of time for Mary and Francis to rear a family. Mary wrote happily to her mother on the day of her wedding. It was the moment for which her mother had planned and for which her uncles had educated her, and when Francis succeeded to the throne, Scotland and France would be united under one crown.

In November, 1558, Mary I, the Catholic Queen of England, died, and was succeeded by the Protestant Queen Elizabeth. Mary Stuart through her grandmother, Henry VIII's sister, was next in succession if Elizabeth had no children; she was moreover a Catholic. Henry II saw the tempting prospect of England as well as Scotland becoming a part of the kingdom of France. Accordingly he ordered that Mary's arms should show those of Scotland, France and England, and that she should be styled Queen of all three countries when she and Francis succeeded to the French throne. Mary agreed happily and obediently. Her position was assured and her future dazzling, but her use of the arms of England gave great offence not only to the English ambassador in France, but to Elizabeth herself.

It is easy to forget, when recalling the long reign of Elizabeth and the affection she came to inspire in the English people, that when she came to the throne as a young woman of twenty-five, the country was split by religion, and her hold on it was precarious. To her Protestant subjects she offered the only hope of their religion being restored. Her Catholic subjects saw her not only as

REGINA · ✝ MARIA · IACOBI · SCOTORVM · REGIS · FILIA · SCOTORVMQVE · NVNC

Plate 3
Mary Queen of Scots at the time of her marriage to Francis. Engraving by Pieter van der Heyden. (Scottish National Portrait Gallery, Edinburgh.)

illegitimate, but as bringing with her the threat of the persecution and suppression of their religion, as the Protestants had been persecuted in the reign of her sister, Mary. The Queen of Scots, with the might of France behind her and regarded by many as the lawful heir, was an ever-present threat to Elizabeth.

It is unlikely that the young Queen-Dauphiness troubled herself with these considerations, and the political move by her father-in-law merely meant to her that a new coat of arms had to be ordered from the court embroiderer for the canopy over her chair of estate, and her silver re-engraved. The long war with Spain had ended, there were increasing numbers of French Protestants, but life at court continued in its sumptuous extravagant way, each ceremony attended by pageantry, at which the royal family and the courtiers wore the most costly and elaborate garments to emphasise their high position.

FRANCISCVS HENRICI II GALLORV REGIS CHRISTIANISS: FILIVS: AC D: FAVENTE CLEMENTIA DELPHINVS

COCK EXCVD

Plate 4
Francis II King of France
(1544–60) as Dauphin.
Engraving by Pieter van der
Heyden. (Scottish National
Portrait Gallery, Edinburgh.)

In the year following the marriage of Mary and Francis, the king's sister, Madame Marguerite, married the Duke of Savoy. Before the wedding and in honour of the event, a tournament was held. On June 30th, 1559, the King, who loved to ride and joust, took part, wearing black and white, the colours of Diane de Poitiers. At the end of the day Henry decided to ride once more against the captain of his archers, a Scot named Montgomery, who accepted reluctantly. Catherine, watching from the pavilion, had a premonition of disaster. She received a message from the King that he would break one more lance in honour of his wife, a belated gesture after her years of silently accepted slights. Before the eyes of the horrified court, Montgomery, instead of breaking his opponent's lance, as the rules required, accidently pierced the king's eye. Ten days later Henry was dead and at last the Guise ambitions were fully realised. Francis II was King, and their niece, to whom he was devoted, was Queen of France.

Catherine de Medici became nominally Regent, but the Guises declared her son of an age to rule, and themselves became the real rulers of France.

Whatever Catherine may have felt about the domination of the Guises, she concealed her thoughts as she had concealed them during the long years of Diane's domination of her husband and the court. She and Mary were constantly together, although now Mary took precedence of her mother-in-law. It is unlikely that they kept their conversation merely to a discussion of the embroidery designs that Catherine took pleasure in working. Both were well educated women, both were intelligent, and Mary was maturing rapidly. It is inconceivable that she did not learn from her mother-in-law some of the ways in which an intelligent woman could overcome the handicap of her sex and exert power in the government of the country: ways in which she could support her feeble, less intelligent husband, for whom both Catherine and Mary, each in her own way, had great affection. Yet Catherine had learned over the years a monumental patience, and had been schooled from childhood in diplomacy and intrigue. Mary, in spite of her gentleness, was impetuous, and had all the assurance which came from a royal upbringing, natural charm and good looks.

However, Catherine's training of her daughter-in-law did not last as long as she had hoped. The year 1560 was a disastrous one for Mary. On June 11th her mother, Marie de Guise, died in Edinburgh, a lonely frugal devout woman, who had struggled to keep the peace between the warring families and the two religions that now divided Scotland, as well as trying to preserve the kingdom for her daughter against the attacks of England. Mary was overcome by grief at the news. On July 6th the Scottish Parliament signed a peace treaty with England in Edinburgh, the English insisting that in return for the evacuation of English troops, those of the King and Queen of France must also leave, and that Mary and Francis should cease to use the arms of England. This was sent to France for their signature, but before it was signed, more ominous news came from Scotland. The Scottish Parliament had passed laws making the Reformed Religion the official religion of Scotland. This was contrary to most other European countries in which the Reformed Religion was imposed by the sovereign.

The final blow fell at the end of the year. Francis caught a chill out hunting, became ill, and in spite of tender nursing by his young wife, died on December 5th, a month before his seventeenth birthday. The hopes of Mary and the Guises were shattered.

Francis was succeeded by his brother, Charles IX, who was only eleven. Catherine at last became Regent in fact as well as in name. Mary, like Catherine, was now Queen Dowager of France. She was entitled to remain there: she could have lived on the estates settled on her at her marriage. Charles IX, although so much younger than Mary, was devoted to her, and perhaps on this account Catherine did not encourage her to remain at court. Mary was young, marriageable and still Queen of Scotland. Rather against her uncles' advice she decided to return to her own kingdom.

She applied to Elizabeth for permission to travel through England to her kingdom, but Elizabeth, aware that this would mean receiving the Scottish Queen who had so recently claimed the English throne and adopted the arms of England, refused safe-conduct. Undaunted, Mary set out on the six-hundred-mile journey by sea, accompanied by Scottish and French ladies and gentlemen and her four Maries. As the four ships left the shores of France Mary wept bitterly, murmuring 'Adieu France, adieu France'.

3 Needlework in France

Mary had arrived in France at a most impressionable age, prepared by her mother to accept that France was the most beautiful country in the world. The royal castles, still in the fever of rebuilding and redecoration that had begun in the reign of Francis I, were still being embellished by Henry II, and after he died, by his widow, Catherine de Medici. Mary saw Amboise, Chenonceaux, Chambord; she saw Fontainebleau, which Francis had transformed from a small hunting lodge into a palace fit to lodge an emperor. She saw Anet, that enchanting castle built by Diane de Poitiers, a castle that was visited with pleasure not only by the King but by his children. She saw them with the stone still fresh, the carvings sharp and clean, and the colours of the paintwork on walls and woodwork rich and glowing. The renaissance decoration of the interiors reflected the taste of French kings for Italian artists and Italian decoration, a trend which had begun before Catherine's marriage to Henry. Francis I had tried to entice Raphael to France, but he refused. Leonardo da Vinci, however, made the journey and died there in 1519. Catherine, who had been brought up in Florence, that city-republic of artists and craftsmen, whose textiles were famous, and whose embroideries were designed by artists, brought her own energy and taste to the decoration of the royal castles.

The textile furnishings of the period have now mostly worn out or been dispersed. Some of the tapestry hangings are still to be found in museums, but the riches of the embroidered furnishings can only be imagined from pictures and the fragments that survive.

The soft furnishings of the court were made and repaired by the *tapissiers*. Originally this name was given to the craftsmen who wove the tapestries in specialist workshops on very large looms, but by the time Mary arrived at the French court, a *tapissier* was one who not only repaired the woven tapestries, but who repaired and made up all the upholstery, lined curtains and hangings, made up pillows and cushions, and put together the stiff elaborate hangings of a four-poster bed, with its upper and lower valances, the upright back panel and the roof or ceiling, all of which were often richly decorated. The state beds were very large by our standards. The English court had several at that time that were eleven feet square. A print depicting the death of Henry II, surrounded by his sorrowing wife and children, and also Mary, shows him lying on such a bed, with a shaped valance embroidered with masks and scrolls.

The valances were often richly decorated with embroidery, and because these were stretched round the top of the bed, they have survived in greater numbers than the curtains, cushions and covers that of necessity received more wear. The court embroiderers, who were usually men, were responsible for the needlework on furnishings. Designs were drawn out on linen or canvas, stretched on a rectangular frame. When large numbers were required, as they must have been when the royal palaces were being rebuilt, some of the furnishings had to be commissioned from professional workshops in Paris. These furnishings would then be mounted by the *tapissier* to fit the particular bed or wooden wall panel.

Since the designs were always commissioned from the embroiderer, the pieces could be unique and personal: the coat of arms or the repeated initials of the owner, or his patron saint. This had been so throughout the preceding century, but the cultivated taste of Francis I and Henry II required decoration in the manner of the Italian Renaissance. Stiff Gothic figures were out of fashion, and the tapestries and embroideries as well as the paintings on the walls were of scenes from the Greek and Roman classics: gods and goddesses, drawn freely from life, sometimes, indeed, portraits. They were bordered by patterns of intricate interlaced ribbons, now called *strapwork*. Instead of the traditional border of flowers and fruit, similar to those on medieval illuminated *Books of Hours*, there now appeared representations of classical sculpture with masks, often grotesque, of men and beasts. In Florence artists could be found to draw out embroidery designs, and a splendid set of church embroideries by Antonio Pollaiuolo can still be seen there in the Cathedral Museum.

In France, this type of figure drawing was beyond the skill of most embroidery designers, so they were forced to rely on books of woodcuts or engravings to achieve the correct proportions and stance of these new and life-like figures. Fortunately these books were appearing in Italy, France and the Netherlands in ever-increasing numbers. They were eagerly bought as the new learning spread and more and more people, particularly women, learnt to read the classics, even if they only read the stories of Ovid, Aesop and Virgil in translation.

These embroidered furnishings could be worked on canvas. Tapestry was slow to weave, and very costly. A passable imitation could be made by an embroiderer, once the design was sketched out on the canvas, by working it in coloured wools, in a half-cross stitch (called *petit point* in French or *tent stitch* in English after the *tenter* or frame on which the canvas was stretched). Although a large piece took time to complete, it was quicker than woven tapestry, for the woven foundation was already provided by the canvas. Moreover, more than one person could work at the same time on a large frame, and as the stitch is simple, it could be done by an unskilled person under supervision.

Even quicker, giving a bold and theatrical effect, appliqué designs (patchwork) could be used. Strapwork borders, quarterings on coats of arms or even garments on the figures depicted on panels could all be cut out of rich materials (damasks or cloth of gold, too expensive and scarce to be used as a ground), and applied to the foundation of velvet, silk or satin, mounted on a backing of linen for firmness. This technique was not new. It had been used on church vestments for over a century.

Plate 5
Part of a hanging, probably for a bed. Yellow satin embroidered with coloured silks.
Framed scene of Europa and the Bull, surrounded by figures, swags and fishes. (The
Metropolitan Museum, New York, Rogers Fund.)

Direct embroidery, using silks and metal thread on silk or satin was perhaps
the most exacting technique for a skilled embroiderer, since the ground material
had to be of a strength to support the stitchery and the dyed silks and gold used
for the embroidery had to be of a delicacy that would not mar its lustre.

One such piece survives, which gives some suggestion of the splendour and
elegance of court furnishings during Mary's stay in France. Probably a bed
hanging, it is of rich yellow satin, and shows scenes embroidered in delicately
coloured silks from Ovid's *Metamorphoses*, including Europa and the Bull,
Diana and Acteon, Daphne and Apollo. Although it may have been made just
after Mary left France, the design, decorated with swags and masks, is typical
of French taste of the Renaissance. The small pictures are taken from an edition
of the *Metamorphoses* first published at Lyons in 1557 by Jean de Tournes.

This was illustrated by Bernard Salomon, and must have been enormously popular with its illustrations of long-limbed, elegant goddesses, for they were reproduced in many editions.

The Countess of Shrewsbury (Bess of Hardwick) was to choose the same scene of Europa and the Bull for a panel on which her initials E S are prominently displayed. It may even have been selected with Mary's help. The draw-

Plate 7
Embroidered panel. Europa and the Bull with the initials E S for Elizabeth, Countess of Shrewsbury. Now at Hardwick Hall, Derbyshire. (The National Trust and the Victoria and Albert Museum, Crown Copyright.)

Left

Plate 8

George, 5th Lord Seton (1531–86), one of the Queen's most loyal supporters and the brother of Mary Seton, one of her Maries. Painted by an unknown French painter at the time of Mary's marriage to the Dauphin. (Scottish National Portrait Gallery, Edinburgh.)

Above

Plate 9

Marie D'Assigny, Madame de Canaples (1502–58), wearing sleeves decorated with blackwork. Painted by F. Clouet. (National Gallery of Scotland, Edinburgh.)

Left

Plate 10

Marie de Guise (1515–60), wife of James V of Scotland, mother of Mary Queen of Scots. Painted by Corneille de Lyon. (Scottish National Portrait Gallery, Edinburgh.)

ing of the figures in the Hardwick panel is closer to the Salomon woodcut than in the French embroidery, but the yellow satin panel echoes the decoration of the whole page on which picture and verse are printed. The border of the page is filled with a delicately grotesque fantasy.

On the satin bed hangings the dwarfs and grotesques of the woodcut have been changed into figures and creatures. The tortoise, crab and fish, whose significance now eludes us, appear in the borders of other pages, but the canopies with suspended swags, the masks and attendant figures are drawn with such assurance that it has been suggested by Edith Standen of the Metropolitan Museum, New York, that the panel, like the book, originated in Lyons, a city noted for its silks even more than for its printing. The design may indeed have been drawn out by Bernard Salomon himself, who is known to have designed silks, or by one of his pupils. These fragments offer some suggestion of the freshness, the colour and the imagination that Mary must have seen in the furnishings of the royal palaces of France.

It was against this background that the human figures – King, Queen and courtiers – moved. Their costume had to be worthy of the setting. The King, source of all advancement, was pre-eminent; the Queen and the royal children also wore clothes of suitable magnificence to emphasise their royal rank. Those who attended the court spent a fortune on clothes in order to proclaim their nobility, and their followers also had to be worthily attired. Pages and other attendants wore livery adorned with the arms or symbols of their masters, not only to be suitably dressed, but also to show by their numbers the extent of their master's establishment. Width and fullness of garments were used to emphasise the importance of the wearer, materials were costly, and the addition of jewels, gold and embroidery added richness to the whole effect.

This attitude to dress was not, of course, confined to the French court. In England, Henry VIII had not stinted money on personal adornment. His daughter, Elizabeth, throughout her reign, however parsimonious she was in other things, arrayed herself in the richest, stiffest, most uncomfortable gowns in order to dazzle the beholders and proclaim her sovereign state. The young Queen of Scots learned early that magnificence of dress was required of a monarch, even though in her case the money for it had to be squeezed from a country that was poor and distant.

From the accounts of the merchants who supplied her in 1551 it is possible to glimpse the splendour of her wardrobe. Perhaps the visit of her mother to France that year necessitated extra expenditure so that the little Queen of Scots could be displayed with pride. The items vary from the touching:

24 ells of fine white silk braid to tie up the hair of the Queen of Scots . . . 10 sols to the bill presented by Nicholas Arnoul, a merchant at Blois, who supplied the most costly materials:

1 ell of cloth of gold
1⅓ ells of cloth of silver
at 43 écus d'or soleil an ell,

for two *davans de cotte* (the part of a petticoat that showed in the front opening of a gown). The accounts also reveal, for instance, that the young Queen wore drawers, sometimes of fine wool, sometimes of cambric – garments that were not common in England at that time, and were still considered improper by Samuel Pepys a century later. Her hosier supplied hose (*chausses*) in a variety of colours, made of material, not knitted. But the word *chausses* also could mean breeches, and Mary appears to have adopted the even more daring and progressive fashion of wearing breeches of Florentine serge, made by her tailor, and worn beneath her skirts for riding. The fashion is said to have been introduced from Italy by Catherine de Medici, who was herself an accomplished rider, and in her youth had been one of the *petite bande* of court ladies who hunted with Francis I, her father-in-law.

Other material supplied to the Queen of Scots in 1551 included twenty ells and a quarter of black velvet at 8 livres 10 sols an ell, in two pieces, some of which was taken to edge a black taffeta gown and make a collar, the rest to be kept to make other clothes when the need arose. Some of it was given to the king's embroiderer, Pierre Danjou, who worked a little hat for Mary, and three sets of sleeves and petticoat fronts. These he decorated with a design of leaves and roses in gold thread: one set for Mary, one for the Princess Elizabeth and one for the Princess Claude, who shared the same nursery. In addition the embroiderer did other work for the young Queen. A cape of Florence serge had a gold-embroidered border: red taffeta was quilted for sleeves; satin was garnished with gold and pearls for a head dress; crimson velvet covered with silver thread for the front of a petticoat and a pair of sleeves; a band of black velvet was embroidered with silver thread 'to the depth of three fingers', with sleeves to match, to which were attached fifteen round buttons of gold taffeta.

There is also payment to the embroiderer for a favour of white silk, a gift from Mary to the Dauphin, with a fanciful border of fifes and the 'devices' of Mary and Francis. Perhaps the 'devices' included their initials: the Greek φ for Francis, and ΧΧ for Mary, later to be superimposed and used as her cipher on her signet ring.

A crayon portrait of Mary at that age, now in the Musée Condé, Chantilly, France, does no more than suggest some of the finery mentioned in the accounts. In it she wears a jewelled and embroidered cap covering her neatly parted hair. The stiff bodice has a border of embroidery in the form of strapwork, perhaps in silver thread, across the front of the yoke and down the front opening. Her shoulders and neck are modestly covered with a sheer material: the sleeves are slashed and embroidered. In a later portrait by Clouet, when she was fifteen, she is dressed in simple white; a later one, also by Clouet, shows her again in white, this time worn as royal mourning for Henry II. Indeed the portraits of Mary, unlike the many of Elizabeth of England, give scarcely a hint of the richness and gaiety of her dress as glimpsed in the accounts and inventories both in France and Scotland.

At her wedding, it was noted, she wore shimmering white, ablaze with diamonds. No portrait in this dress survives, but her Master of Household, George, Lord Seton, brother of Mary Seton, was one of the Commissioners sent by the Scottish Parliament to witness the wedding. In his portrait he is shown in the suit he probably wore on that day: scarlet doublet and hose embroidered with strapwork in gold thread, enclosing golden thistles. On his scarlet wand of office are the crowned initials of his sovereign ΜR.

4 Ladies' 'works'

Even with so much professional embroidery available it was still considered necessary for the young Queen to be taught to sew and to embroider. In the same year (1551) that so much money had been expended on clothing the sum of 32 sols was laid out for the purchase of worsteds (twisted woollen yarn) for the Queen of Scots to 'learn to make works'. Ladies' 'works' – sewing – was regarded as a necessary accomplishment for all women, even queens, and although two pounds of wool sounds a formidable amount for a girl of nine to use, even if she were taught knitting as well, it may be that the wool came in assorted colours, to encourage her in the use of tent stitch and cross stitch, the stitches she most commonly used later in life.

No doubt Mary and the young Princesses were encouraged in their needlework by Catherine de Medici, who had learned her skill as a child in Florence in the Convent of the Murate. There the nuns had, for nearly a century, been renowned for the excellence of their embroidery, some of which still survives in the parish church of San Gimignano. The needlework that Catherine learned there remained a source of pleasure to her in her years as Queen, just as it remained a solace to her daughter-in-law, and her appreciation of the skills involved caused her to protect and encourage lacemakers and embroiderers. In 1551 Catherine and Henry founded *L'Atelier de la Trinité* in Paris, a school for poor children to learn all the textile arts and become skilled workers. Although Catherine is reported to have spent her afternoons 'working in silks', she appears to have been fascinated by the intricacies of *lacis* (*filet brodé* or darned netting). When she died in 1589, nearly a thousand squares of this lace were said to have been found in boxes among her possessions. For *lacis* a square of net, knotted like a fishing net, is stretched on a square frame and darned with a needle and thread. The pattern is made by filling in the meshes or leaving them open. To be worked correctly the thread must run under and over in a pre-arranged pattern, rather like a maze, so that the thread does not cross a square intended to be empty.

The working-out of a design for *lacis* is something of a puzzle and requires ingenuity and application, unlike tent stitch, the monotony of which can be soothing. The pattern has to be planned on squared paper beforehand, as the design cannot be marked on the net. Designs were usually simple and geometrical: flowers, birds and animals were popular with the domestic needlewoman. Larger pieces tended to be too complicated, and also required larger frames. Small frames were easily portable, and the designs for them less daunting. When completed the squares could be joined together to make large hangings, even bed hangings. At Chenonceaux in 1603 after the death of Catherine there was a *lit de réseuil* (bed of network) in the mourning chamber of Louise de Lorraine, with the prayer desk under black draperies covered with white network.

It is not surprising, therefore, that the earliest needlework pattern books intended for the domestic needlewoman, not the professional, should show patterns in squares for this type of lace. One of the earliest, *Il Burato* published in Italy in 1527, was intended for darned lace of this type, but worked on woven linen gauze (*buratto,* a stiff material used for sieves) instead of a knotted net. One of the most popular of these books, which ran into several editions and was copied in other countries, was published in Paris in 1587 by Frédéric Vinciolo, described as a Venetian, to whom Catherine is said to have given exclusive rights to manufacture the enormous starched lace ruffs which she made fashionable in France. Vinciolo's pattern book *Singuliers et nouveaux pourtraicts* (Unusual and new designs) included among the laces a section of patterns for *lacis*, detailing the number of meshes in each direction for easier working. They show flowers, animals and birds with the fashionable goddesses to represent Spring and Summer.

Darned net and tent and cross stitch in wool were not, however, enough for a young girl's education in needlework. Plain sewing had to be mastered for the making of linen garments, such as shifts and shirts, also bed and table linen. The young Queen's accounts for 1551 include that of Estienne Gangan, *Marchand Linger* (merchant linen draper) who supplied fine linen and silk crêpe to be made up for the Queen's use, although fourteen shirts for her pages appear to have been supplied ready-made. Rather surprisingly he also supplied a Turkey carpet for the queen's room.

On the other hand a separate bill was sent in by Agatha Burgensis, the *lingère,* who made up six nightdresses trimmed with ruffs and back stitch, as well as linen sheets, covers and chemises or shifts. She practised a craft which, unlike that of the professional embroiderer, was not male-dominated. The *lingère* in France, the maker-up and embroiderer of fine underwear, sheer handkerchiefs and delicate bed linen, has to the present day retained an identity separate from that of the embroiderer, tailor or dressmaker. But the fine sewing and embroidered linen supplied by the *lingère* was only a fraction of the requirements of the Queen and her household: the rest had to be made up by her maids and ladies. Every woman had to be able to take part in the making up of her own personal and household linen. Every little girl had to learn to hem before she learned to embroider.

As well as bed linen and shifts Agatha Burgensis also supplied the Queen with two pairs of sleeves, one embroidered with gold thread and crimson silk, the other pair embroidered with silver and black silk. Decorated undergarments were not a new fashion, but it had become elegant to emphasise the whiteness of the linen by a delicate line embroidery, in a dark colour, usually black. A pair of such sleeves is worn by Madame de Canaples in the portrait by Clouet. She had been, like Catherine de Medici, one of Francis I's *petite*

Plate 11
Panel of *lacis* (filet brodé, darned net), made up of joined rectangles. 16th century. (The Royal Scottish Museum, Edinburgh.)

bande – the young ladies of the French court who hunted with that energetic, cultivated and pleasure-loving monarch. The story is told that on one occasion he presented each of his *petite bande* with nine ells of damask for a gown. To Madame de Canaples he presented eleven ells, so even in her youth she must have been a big girl.

The stitch employed for the decoration of linen with black silk was usually *double running*, or, as it is sometimes called, *Holbein stitch*, since so many of the sitters in Holbein's portraits wear shirts, shifts, collars or wrist frills decorated with this type of blackwork. It is simple to do. The gaps in the running stitch which outlines the geometrical line are covered by the running stitches on the return journey. It is worked, like *lacis,* by counting the threads, a process which the hand-woven linen of the period made far easier than does the closer, machine-woven linen of today. Early pattern books intended for the domestic needlewoman printed patterns for double running – or Spanish stitch as it was called by the German Quentel in 1527 – as well as the squared designs for *lacis.* As in *lacis* for all except very simple designs the course must be plotted before embarking on the work in order that all the small branches or flowers are covered before the needle begins its return journey. It appealed especially, therefore, to the needlewoman in an age that enjoyed mazes, anagrams and emblems.

Thus by her background and her education Mary was expected, like all girls, to have a knowledge of needlework and skill to undertake it. It is somewhat surprising that there appears to be no record of her making any small personal gifts with her needle, for her mother or for anyone else. Elizabeth of England, when young, made gifts for her father, Henry VIII, and for Katherine Parr, her stepmother. These were exercises in translation, written on vellum

Plate 12
Detail of the panel.

Plate 13
Design for a panel of *lacis* from F. Vinciolo *Singuliers et nouveaux pourtraicts* first published in 1587. (The National Library of Scotland, Edinburgh.)

in her elegant clear hand and bound in home-made embroidered covers, incorporating the recipients' initials. They are charming and intensely personal gifts made by a schoolgirl, costing very little except for time and labour. Such thrifty presents may not, of course, have been considered suitable for a reigning queen, because jewels and gold chains were expected. Even the favour she gave the Dauphin was professionally embroidered.

Instead she was expected to encourage the needlework of others. She is said to have founded a school of needlework. Two of her mother's sisters were abbesses, one of the convent of St. Pierre, Reims, the other, Antoinette, of the famous Benedictine Abbey of Faremoutiers. On her mother's instructions she sent them some of her outgrown dresses for vestments: one dress to the Abbess of St. Pierre, two of the Abbess of Faremoutiers. The material of the dresses was not specified. If it were cloth of gold or silver, it could have been cut up

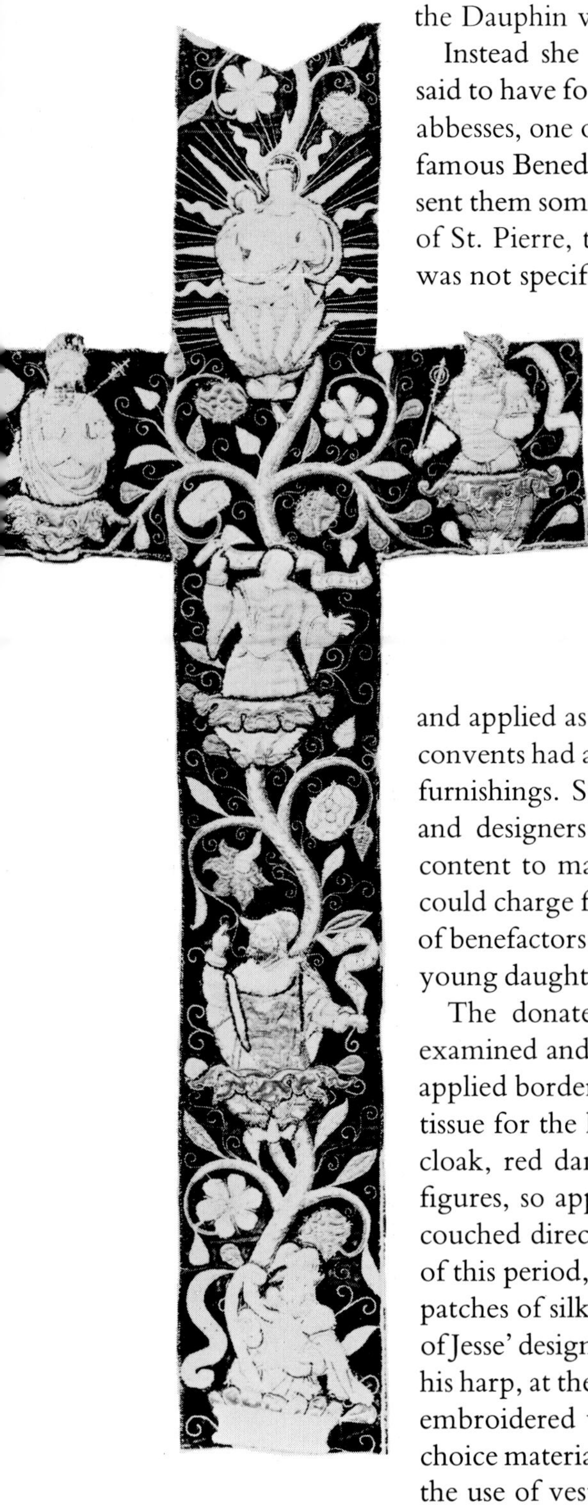

Plate 14
Part of an orphrey. Applied silks and gold tissue on a red silk ground. The design shows part of the Tree of Jesse, the ancestors of the Virgin: David at the base with his harp, Solomon above David. Solomon wears a blue silk tunic decorated with the lilies of France. (The Victoria and Albert Museum, Crown Copyright.)

and applied as part of the decoration of a new chasuble or altar frontal. Many convents had a workroom for the making and repairing of vestments and altar furnishings. Some, like the Murate Convent in Florence, had the resources and designers to undertake commissions for other churches. Others were content to make and repair their own. Those who undertook commissions could charge for their services and materials, the others had to rely on the gifts of benefactors and the faithful. In this case Marie de Guise was encouraging her young daughter to play the part of a modest benefactor to her sisters' convents.

The donated garments would be unpicked, and the material carefully examined and sorted. Widths from skirts could be used to make a handsome applied border. Even small patches could be utilised to enrich vestments: gold tissue for the haloes and breastplates of saints, blue velvet for the Madonna's cloak, red damask for a martyr's tunic and smaller scraps for flowers. The figures, so applied, would be embellished by scrolls of gold or silver thread couched directly on to the silk or velvet of the background. A French piece of this period, an orphrey, now in the Victoria and Albert Museum, has small patches of silks and gold tissue applied to give colour and liveliness to a 'Tree of Jesse' design, showing the pedigree of the Virgin and her son. David, holding his harp, at the base of the stem, is below Solomon, who wears a blue silk tunic embroidered with the golden lilies of France. This method of using old but choice material was not confined to convents. Later in her life Mary sanctioned the use of vestments to secular use. As Queen of France she had no need for economy; she could afford to be charitable over the disposal of her wardrobe.

SCOTLAND

5 The Queen of Scots

Mary landed at Leith, the port of Edinburgh, on Tuesday, August 19th, 1561, with a sea-fog, the *haar*, obscuring the coasts of the country she had left as a child. Although this was regarded as an evil portent by those accompanying her, it was more symbolic of the hazy recollections Mary retained of the appearance of her native land. She was as eager to see her kingdom as her subjects were to see their barely remembered Queen. The citizens of Edinburgh greeted her with pleasure and enthusiasm. They saw an elegant and charming girl, about six feet tall, who rode superbly, and was as anxious to please them as she had been to charm the court of France. To modern eyes her portraits do not convey the beauty that so enchanted those who saw her, but her slender height, red gold hair, and fine skin as well as her attractive voice and eager charm all combined to give the impression of a most beautiful Princess. Even John Knox, leader of the Scottish Reformation and her most implacable enemy, grudgingly described her appearance as pleasing.

Before her arrival Mary had given her assurance that Calvinism established by the Scottish Parliament should continue without hindrance, whilst she herself would hear Mass in the privacy of her palace. The warmth of their welcome did not prevent the outspoken citizens of Edinburgh from demonstrating against the celebration of Mary's first Mass, at which some of her Guise relatives were present. A servant preparing for the ceremony was attacked by an angry mob as he crossed the palace courtyard. They seized the candlesticks and broke up the candles. In spite of this Mary continued her policy of religious toleration, and in this she was supported by her older half-brother, Lord James Stewart, to whom she now looked for support and advice.

Lord James, the illegitimate son of James V and Lady Margaret Douglas, had become a Protestant, and was accepted by the English as the chief Scottish negotiator: indeed he was secretly subsidised by them to ensure the continuance of Protestantism in Scotland. He had accompanied Mary from France, and she looked to him for the same consideration and support that her maternal relatives the Guises had given her in France.

The situation, however, was scarcely comparable. Her Guise uncles had brought her up to be the obedient instrument of their political aspirations as the wife of the French King. Lord James, although her nearest relative and elder brother, himself had a claim to the Scottish throne, if only his illegitimate birth could conveniently be disproved. His influence over Mary and her dependence upon him would be drastically reduced if she took another husband.

And it was obvious that she should marry in order to provide an heir, not only to the Scottish throne, but also to that of England, since Elizabeth seemed in no hurry to marry herself.

At first Mary tried to learn the day-to-day politics of her kingdom, from which she had hitherto been sheltered. She attended the deliberations of her Council. Remembering perhaps how Catherine de Medici had embroidered each afternoon while listening to the conversation around her, Mary sat in the council chamber with her head bent over a piece of needlework, listening with her expression hidden. Her mind was more upon the Scottish accents she heard around her than upon her stitches. The English envoy, Thomas Randolph, was sufficiently impressed by this feminine ruse to report it in a letter he sent on October 24th, 1561: 'I was sent for into the Council Chamber, where she herself ordinarily sitteth the most part of the time, sowing at some work or another.'

The intricacies of Scottish politics were not confined to the split between Catholics and the newly established Protestants, nor to diplomacy between England and Scotland, each suspicious of the other after centuries of war. They were bedevilled by family feuds and rivalries of the nobles, many of them Stewart relations of Mary. These must have been as difficult for her to grasp, and even more to control, as they are for us to understand at this distance in time. The noble families were activated by a great greed for power and for land, both of which were the sovereign's to give or take. A disgraced noble could be deprived of possessions, land and life. The man who had helped to overthrow him could be rewarded with his estates, which had reverted to the crown. The system was not peculiar to Scotland: in England Elizabeth with her needle-sharp intelligence and acute money-sense kept all perquisites firmly in her own hands, awarding them with diplomatic skill. Mary – young, spoilt and generous – was completely unprepared for the political realities of her own kingdom.

The royal residences – Holyroodhouse and the castle in Edinburgh, Stirling Castle, Linlithgow and Falkland palaces and Lochleven Castle – must have seemed disappointingly cramped and austere after the magnificent castles of France. Mary had brought beds and hangings, tapestries, cushions and linen with her. These were in the charge of her French chamberlain, Servais de Condé, together with others (some rather shabby) that had been used by her mother, who had been little interested in maintaining a display of royal magnificence during her long widowhood. Two professional embroiderers, Pierre Oudry and Ninian Miller, were on her staff, and three *tapissiers* (upholsters rather than tapestry workers): Pierre Martin, Nicholas Carbonier and David Liages. With great energy the staff began to make the royal residences comfortable, even if they fell short of the splendour that Mary had known previously. Bed hangings with valances and curtains were made not only for the four Maries, but for her women and even for the queen's female fool, Jardinière. Some were embroidered or decorated with appliqué of silk or gold tissue, others were trimmed with *silkin passmentis* (silken braid).

The climate, with its dense sea-mists even in August, must have seemed bitterly cold after France. The bed hangings of Mary's women were of warm woollen *plading* (a plain, not a tartan material), trimmed with a worsted fringe. Even the silk beds with damask or taffeta hangings had their curtains and canopies lined with *sarge* (fine woollen) to keep out the cold and damp.

It cannot be assumed, however, that Mary herself took any active part in the decoration of these soft furnishings. The accounts for expenses and materials used by the *tapissiers* and embroiderers were brought to her quarterly for her signature to authorize payment, but she had too many duties to perform to undertake the embroidery of the many large pieces that are now hopefully attributed to her during this period of her life.

As in France the court travelled from one residence to another, if only in the interests of cleanliness. Of all her Scottish palaces Linlithgow alone appears to have been equipped (perhaps on her mother's initiative) with a built-in primitive form of water-closet. At all the others Mary and her ladies were obliged to use a *close-stool* or commode hung with velvet or damask. As well as visiting each of her residences in turn Mary took every opportunity to explore as much of her kingdom as possible. These journeys on horseback satisfied her need for outdoor exercise. Whatever its other deficiencies Scotland also offered superb opportunities for her favourite sports: hunting, hawking and archery. She kept the deerhounds and terriers she had loved as a child in France. She sent one to France as a gift, complete with black velvet collar.

Indoors the young Queen was equally energetic. Like Elizabeth she loved dancing, and John Knox thundered against this hellish occupation from the pulpit of the High Kirk of St. Giles. Undeterred the Queen organised entertainments and parties at which she and her ladies danced – often in costume, for she loved dressing up. She caused gossip when she and her Maries, dressed as men, darted among the citizens of Edinburgh incognito. Her long legs must have made the disguise plausible.

Marriages in the court were an opportunity for royal entertainments. When Lord James Stewart, whom she had made Earl of Moray, married Lady Agnes Keith, daughter of the Earl Marischal, in 1562, the banquets continued for three days. Perhaps Mary recalled with nostalgia the splendour of the entertainments at her own wedding in Paris. It was becoming increasingly important for her to marry again.

There was no lack of suitors for so eligible a bride. Indeed, one of her own subjects, Sir John Gordon, son of the powerful and Catholic Earl of Huntly, threatened to kidnap her in order to marry her. But in rebelling against the Queen, both father and son died: the Earl of Huntly by a merciful heart attack on the battlefield of Corrichie, Aberdeenshire, and his son by being beheaded, the latter in the presence of the Queen. Marriage to a Catholic would have offended Queen Elizabeth, and would have impeded her succession to the throne of England. Moreover her own nobles would not have allowed one of their peers to become King Consort, as Mary was later to discover for herself.

In the end she fell in love with another claimant to the throne of England. The eighteen-year-old Henry, Lord Darnley, son of the Earl of Lennox, was descended from Mary's grandmother, Margaret Tudor, a sister of Henry VIII. Margaret Tudor's second husband was sixth Earl of Angus, and their daughter, Margaret, Countess of Lennox, was Darnley's mother. Darnley arrived in

Plate 15
James Stewart, Earl of
Moray (1531–70), half-
brother of Mary Queen of
Scots. He wears a shirt
decorated with blackwork
embroidery. Detail of a
portrait by H. Eworth. (The
Earl of Moray.)

Scotland, ostensibly with Elizabeth's permission, in February, 1565. On July 29th, Mary and Darnley were married privately in the chapel of Holyrood-house. He was four years younger than the Queen, tall and handsome, and she appeared very much in love with him. She wore deep mourning for the ceremony, to symbolise her widowed state, and only after it was over did she change into a more joyful costume. Mary conferred the title of King on Darnley but this was never confirmed by the Scottish Parliament, so inept and arrogant was he.

Elizabeth was furious, especially when she heard the marriage had been celebrated by a Catholic priest. Two Catholics, even if one were merely nominal in his adherence to the faith, each with a claim to the English throne, would be a very real temptation to the dissident Catholics of England to depose or assassinate Elizabeth. James Stewart, Earl of Moray, Mary's half-brother, saw his influence over the Queen diminishing. In addition, he disliked Darnley intensely. Darnley was greedy, coarse and arrogant, and Moray had no difficulty in persuading other Protestant lords of the dangers of the marriage and in raising a rebellion. He was outlawed by Mary, who, in high fettle, rode with Darnley at the head of her troops against the rebel lords in what was called the Chaseabout Raid, for they never actually encountered each other, and the rebels escaped to seek safety in England.

Mary's son and heir, James, was born on June 15th, 1566. Her pregnancy was by no means a quiet time of rest and embroidery: on the contrary, the most bitter strife had arisen between the Queen and her husband. Although Mary was enamoured of him on her marriage, it had become obvious that to Darnley Mary was merely the means of becoming King of Scotland and eventually of England also. Mary had granted him the title of King, but only the Scottish Parliament could make him King in fact, with the right to rule alone if Mary died in childbirth. Not surprisingly, in view of Darnley's talent for making enemies and his interest in nothing but hunting and hawking, his coronation was indefinitely delayed. The Crown Matrimonial, for which he had married Mary, was denied him.

On their marriage a coin had been struck, a silver ryal (worth about thirty shillings) bearing both their heads, with the inscription *Henricus & Maria D Gra R & R Scotorum* (Henry and Mary by the grace of God King and Queen of Scots). That Darnley's name should take precedence over that of Mary caused great offence, and the Privy Council met on December 22nd, 1565, and laid down exact instructions for the issue of a new ryal. This was to be 'a new penny of silver callit the the Marye ryal . . .' and, so that there should be no mistake, it was enacted that the inscription should begin with 'ane croce (cross) directlie aboun the crown *Maria et Henricus Dei Gratia Regina et Rex Scotorum* (Mary and Henry by the grace of God Queen and King of Scots)'.

In order to drive home the full implication of this change of coin there was an insultingly frank emblem on the other face: '. . . ane palm tre crownit, ane schell padocke crepand up the schank of the samyn' (a palm tree crowned, with a land tortoise creeping up the trunk). The crowned palm tree represented the Queen, the land tortoise Darnley, who by this marriage had hoped to climb from his lowly position. The motto chosen underlined the message: '*Dat Gloria Vires* ('Glory gives strength'), and it was further emphasised around this face of the coin 'begyning at ane thrisell *Expurgat Deus et Dissipentur Inimici Eius* (Arise, Lord, and scatter thine enemies)'. The message for Darnley could hardly have been more pointed. He was unlikely ever to be made King of Scots by Parliament. Once Mary was delivered of a son, his chances of becoming a reigning monarch were even less.

His spite vented itself on David Rizzio, Mary's Italian secretary, who entertained the Queen with his music and by playing at cards with her – a pastime she had enjoyed even in the royal nursery in France. Darnley accused Rizzio of undue familiarity, if not downright immorality with his wife. When Mary

Plate 16
Coin. The 'Mary Ryal', first minted 1566, bearing the emblem of a crowned tree with a land tortoise climbing up the trunk, to show the relative positions of Mary and Darnley at their marriage. (The National Museum of Scottish Antiquities, Edinburgh.)

was five months pregnant, a band of conspirators burst into the queen's supper room at Darnley's instigation, dragged Rizzio into the next room and stabbed him to death.

Believing that her own life and that of her unborn child were in danger Mary fled to the castle of Dunbar, riding pillion behind an equerry through the night for twenty-five miles. Darnley accompanied her, riding savagely and urging her horse on. The conspirators escaped over the border, but they made sure that the Queen knew of her husband's complicity. Moray, who had almost certainly known of the plot to kill Rizzio, returned to her side and was pardoned by his half-sister, who longed for all the support she could command before her coming confinement.

Mary did not forgive Darnley either for his insinuations or for his brutality. After the birth of her son she considered the possibility of a divorce. Darnley was away from the court as much as possible, and even absented himself from his son's christening in December at Stirling, for which Queen Elizabeth, who was a godmother, sent a magnificent gold font. In January Darnley took ill in Glasgow, and hearing of his illness Mary visited him there. She persuaded him to return to Edinburgh for convalescence. This he did, staying in a small house, Kirk o' Field, beside the walls of Edinburgh in order to rest and take baths. There, on the night of Sunday, February 9th, 1567 while Mary was at Holyrood celebrating the marriage of her page, Bastien, the house by the wall was blown up by gunpowder, and the bodies of Darnley and his servant were found lying in the garden, both dead. They had been killed, not by the explosion, but by expert strangulation as they tried to escape in their night-clothes.

6 Lochleven

The citizens of Edinburgh were roused by the noise of the explosion. Their horror, when they learned of the deed, was not lessened by their dislike of the man who had tried to become their King. This horror was echoed in the courts of Europe, especially as the Queen apparently made no effort to pursue those responsible. Elizabeth wrote to Mary immediately afterwards: 'Men say that, instead of seizing the murderers, you are looking through your fingers while they escape'. The scandal became greater when it was learned that Mary, far from punishing the man suspected of being the chief murderer, had within three months married him. He was James Hepburn, Earl of Bothwell, a Protestant and Lord High Admiral of Scotland.

It is true that Bothwell, a powerful border lord, was acquitted of the murder by the Scottish Parliament, although the widowed Queen significantly took no part in the accusation: the accuser was Darnley's father, the Earl of Lennox, who dared not appear in person in an Edinburgh filled with Bothwell's followers. It was widely believed that Bothwell was responsible, and that the Queen herself may have had some knowledge of the plot. These suspicions were strengthened as Bothwell first kept the Queen apparently a prisoner with him at the castle of Dunbar whilst cynically arranging his divorce, then proceeded to marry her according to the Protestant rite at Holyrood on May 15th, 1567.

The citizens of Edinburgh and courts of Europe debated the scandal of the queen's third marriage, and writers ever since have sought to blame or excuse her for this extraordinary action. Some have attributed it entirely to Bothwell's sexual attraction; certainly he had a way with women, although he lacked the long legs and smooth good looks of the young Darnley. Others suggest that as the Queen had been in poor health since the birth of her child, she had married Bothwell in the belief that it was the wish of her nobles, and in the hope of gaining a strong helpmeet who would support her in the arduous task of ruling her factious country. This is certainly the explanation she gave Queen Elizabeth and to Charles IX, her brother-in-law in France. If she believed it herself, it showed how little she had learned since arriving in Scotland, and how much more shrewd were Elizabeth's elaborate evasions of marriage; her refusal to share her throne with any man who would seek to dominate and rule.

The Scottish nobles were outraged, not because the Queen had lost her reputation, for which they cared not a shred, but because she had allowed

Bothwell to seize power through the marriage. Even those who had been implicated in Darnley's murder joined forces against Bothwell and the Queen, and scurrilous lampoons appeared in Edinburgh accusing her of adultery with her husband's murderer.

Exactly one month after their marriage, Mary and Bothwell, with a small band of followers, were confronted by a well-armed force at Carberry Hill, outside Edinburgh. Bothwell fled, escaping abroad to end his days in prison in Denmark. Mary, to the jeers of the people who had once acclaimed her, was made a prisoner and taken back to Edinburgh.

From there, distraught and ill, she was removed at night to Lochleven, a royal castle set on an island in the middle of a loch and held for the Scottish crown by Sir William Douglas. Her captors allowed her no luggage, and she was accompanied only by two of her women. The lords, with the Queen a captive, resumed the government of Scotland.

Here on Lochleven for the next ten and a half months she was kept a prisoner, and it is during this period that she is believed to have worked so many of the large pieces of needlework now attributed to her in Scotland. Her life and the facts as we know them scarcely suggest that she spent her time placidly working large pieces of embroidery. Instead she spent her time writing furious letters and making all kinds of promises in order to obtain her release from so unjust a captivity.

Queen Elizabeth was horrified to learn that the Scots had imprisoned their anointed Queen, and instructed her envoy, Sir Nicholas Throckmorton, to try to see Mary. She was even more alarmed when she heard from him that Mary was offering, in return for her freedom, to go to live quietly in France – or in England. To have the Queen of Scots as her permanent guest in retirement would require some thought, she told Throckmorton. Elizabeth foresaw only too clearly that the presence of their Queen in England would attract not only dissident Scots: as next in line to the English throne she would also become a rallying point for dissident Catholics in England.

Mary begged that, if she were not allowed to be set at liberty, then she might instead be moved to Stirling Castle, where she could be near her baby son, who, according to the custom of the time, was being brought up in the royal nursery there with his own ladies and gentlemen. This was refused. The lords demanded that Mary should divorce the absent Bothwell. She refused to do so, not because she was still devoted to him, but because she was pregnant by him. She pointed out that if she did so, it would make her unborn child illegitimate.

In July she wrote demanding the presence of one of her ladies (she did not specify which), also an apothecary in view of her health, a page, and an embroiderer to 'drawe forth such worke as she would be occupied about'. This last demand was certainly ignored. Her embroiderer, Pierre Oudry, had been rewarded on several occasions for very special service, which must have extended far beyond the mere drawing of her designs on to canvas. The previous December he had received as a gift a complete outfit of 'French black' woollen cloak, doublet and hose trimmed with taffeta, with a leather coat and a fine hat that cost forty shillings.

Whether the apothecary was sent is not clear. The Queen had a miscarriage in the late summer, and was ill and wretched, but one of her Maries, the faithful Mary Seton, was allowed to join her on the island. Believing herself threatened with worse than imprisonment, with death itself, Mary was forced to sign a deed of abdication in favour of her infant son, the year-old James. He was crowned King in the Protestant church at Stirling on July 29th, 1567, and the triumphant Moray was proclaimed Regent. The English envoy was not permitted to visit Mary on Lochleven. A few clothes were grudgingly sent from her large wardrobe. She wrote for further supplies, and the faithful Servais de Condé noted the pathetic list of articles he was permitted to send through her jailers to her island prison.

Only small parcels seem to have been allowed. In July she received two pairs of velvet and two pairs of leather shoes, underwear, a little basket of sweet-meats and a small crimson velvet casket with an F in silver-gilt (bringing memories of her happy life with Francis as Queen of France). With it came a dozen and a half little flowers painted on canvas and outlined in black silk, together with six hanks of twisted black Spanish silk and several hanks of other colours, as well as a packet of smooth silks in assorted colours with which to work the flowers.

These small pieces were to pass the time until the Queen was set at liberty, which she believed would be soon. In August she was allowed to receive another parcel, which contained sweets, pins, a ball of soap for washing her hands, a packet of coloured silks and four hanks each of gold and silver thread, as well as two ells of lawn and two French ells (about two and a half yards) of fine linen to make drawers for the Queen.

In September, as the days got cooler, the Queen wrote imperiously for more clothes for herself and her maidens 'for thai are naikit', shoes, two pairs of sheets, gold and silver thread and any twisted silk that remained, as well as covering for beds 'to put under the tother covering', some prunes and pears. She also wrote: 'Ye shall cause make one dozen of rasene needles and moulds and send me'. In October Servais de Condé noted the dispatch of most of the clothing requested, together with 'des moulles et eguylle pour faire le réseu' (gauges and needles to make netting).

In the winter and early spring time must have hung heavily, although she played cards and took what exercise she could on the small island, while her jailer, Sir William Douglas, and his family continually watched her. She began to smuggle letters out to her relatives in France, to Lord Seton and others who were dissatisfied with the regency of Moray and his friends. She even attempted to escape disguised as a washerwoman, but the boatman, who tried to see her face, which she hid, recognised her beautiful white hands and returned her to the island. At the beginning of May with the help of George Douglas, the impressionable young brother of her jailer, a successful escape was contrived while the family were at supper. Safely across the loch in a small boat Mary was met by Lord Seton, Mary Seton's brother, and a few other faithful followers.

The news of her escape stirred up her opponents as well as her supporters. The opportunities for personal gain under a long Protestant regency while the infant King grew up were balanced against the benefits of rule under a Catholic

Queen who would certainly need another husband. Many nobles and their followers gathered to support the Queen, Moray collected his supporters to defend the rights of the infant King, and only a week after Mary's escape from Lochleven, the battle of Langside, near Glasgow, decided the matter. The queen's forces were defeated, and Mary was forced to gallop south west to avoid capture. Wearing borrowed clothes and in a small fishing boat she sailed away from Scotland across the Solway to seek sanctuary in the neighbouring kingdom of England and her long-awaited meeting with its Queen, Elizabeth.

7 The Queen's movables

Mary had arrived in Scotland in August, 1561, but her French chamberlain, Servais de Condé, did not begin to make an inventory of the *Quenis Movables* until November 25th. This diligent and meticulous servant remained with her until she left Scotland, and stayed on for at least two years afterwards. He deserves our gratitude for his painstaking lists of the textile furnishings in his charge. From them we can learn the materials and the decoration of her chairs of estate, her beds, stools and chapel furnishings, as well as notes on their subsequent renovations. The first inventory must have been dictated, for it is written in Scots and contains such details as:

60. Item. aucht serviottes of vnhemmit great lyning (eight serviettes of unhemmed wide linen).
    – Deliverit to Madam mosel de Ralle (Mlle Rallay, the maid, whom the queen had brought with her from France) to rub the Quenis heid.
61. Item twa sampler pieces of cammes pennit to be sewit.

These two items were from the list of the *Queen Regent's Movables,* left by Mary's mother, Marie de Guise.

On the other hand, when he made out the list of materials given out by him to the queen's *tapissiers* and to her embroiderers, particularly Pierre Oudry, Servais de Condé wrote in French, using his own spelling of the difficult Scottish names: Flammi, Beton, Ceton et Leuiston for Fleming, Beaton, Seton and Livingston, Lifcot for Linlithgow and Faclan for Falkland. His lists, presented to the Queen for her signature quarterly, show that most of the materials in his charge were for furnishings, although he gave out the silks and metal thread to the queen's embroiderers who embroidered her clothes as well as her household furnishings.

Mary must have been dismayed by the threadbare state of her mother's surroundings after the elegance and luxury of the French court. Only three *tapissiers,* Pierre Martin, Nicholas Carbonier and David Liages, are mentioned, and they were at once set to work to make up new furnishing and to renovate the old. In France some ten embroiderers had been employed by the Queen, for their blankets and sheets were carefully listed by Servais de Condé, and then gradually used for other purposes. One sheet was cut up to make handkerchiefs for the queen's fool, Jardinière. Of the twenty beds brought by Mary (the hangings and canopies, not wooden bases), twelve were embroidered: a bed of satin broderie work (appliqué) in four colours of satin (red, blue, yellow and white) bordered with 'false gold' and silver, a bed of crimson velvet enriched with phoenixes of gold and tears, one of black velvet embroidered with arms and spheres and edged with cloth of gold, and yet another of violet-brown velvet with applied cloth of gold and silver, with ciphers and flowers embroidered in silk and gold. There was one of crimson velvet with true lovers' knots and the cipher of Francis, another with the letter A (later called the Bed of Amitie) and two others of equally sumptuous materials with oval compartments showing 'histories', perhaps similar to the yellow satin French bed hanging now in the Metropolitan Museum, New York. All of them appear to have been decorated with applied materials and gold. Only one of the 'auld beddis' had an upper valance sewn with worsted with a design of satyrs and foliage.

Another bed was described as 'a bed all made of broderie work of gold of the history of the works of Hercules furnished with six pands (valances), roof, headpiece and three underpands (lower valances around the base) which is neither stuffed nor garnished'. A note is added to this entry: 'Efterwards furnished (provided with curtains, mattress etc.) in 1566'. Some of these beds were listed as being in Edinburgh Castle in 1578, after Mary had left Scotland. The 'Hercules' bed had by then acquired curtains of gold and crimson silk. It appears to have been taken to England by her son James when he succeeded Elizabeth in 1603, and was still at Hampton Court in 1659, nearly a hundred years after it was listed by Servais de Condé.

The 'Cloths of Estate', those canopies under which the Queen sat to show her royal rank, were equally splendid and richly embroidered. One of green velvet had a 'great tree of personages and shields', another of cloth of gold and violet silk, her parents' arms and crowned ciphers, and another had 'trees, personages, shields and branches of holly'. Surprisingly none of those described appears to bear her own arms or cipher.

Two hangings, said to have come from the Palace of Linlithgow and Lochleven Castle, are preserved in the Royal Scottish Museum. They are of red woollen cloth, with appliqué of black silk, embroidered with black, yellow and blue silk. They are both assured professional pieces and illustrate very well how applied material and stitchery were combined to decorate the hangings required for furnishing. Although the material is not as sumptuous as the silks and velvets listed in the inventories, close examination of the red woollen cloth on which they are worked reveals that originally it had a short lustrous pile, and may have been mistaken for velvet by the clerk making the inventory.

None of the rich textiles of these inventories can now be traced. One or two of the items, such as the cloth of estate of black velvet and a canopy of yellow shot taffeta, together with six pieces of tapestry, are ominously docketed: 'Lost in the King's (Darnley's) lodgings when he died in February 1567'. A set of embroidered hangings, listed as 'tapestry' with the arms of Longueville, her mother's first husband, which must have been brought by Marie de Guise in 1538 on her marriage to James V, were so shabby by 1617 that the Privy Council arranged for them to be patched together for use on King James's return from London for a short visit to his native land.

There were twenty-six cushions to soften the hard wooden chairs and stools:

Plate 17
Red woollen hanging, with applied black silk embroidered with golden yellow silk. From the royal palace of Linlithgow. (Trustees of the Royal Museum of Scotland.)

one of green satin embroidered with little shields and branches, and six of silk lined with red leather. Others were made rapidly. Each chair of estate required several, small as well as large. There were folding stools, quilts, covers (one of violet-brown velvet powdered with fifty gold-embroidered fleurs-de-lys), and sets of embroidered and woven wall hangings, lumped together as 'Tapestries of all sorts'. (This is a confusion as properly tapestry is a figured textile completely woven on a loom. Canvas embroidery ought never to be described as tapestry, but these inventories show how long ago the confusion began.)

From all these bewildering details a picture emerges of the young Queen returning to her scarcely remembered homes, now so shabby and run-down after the twenty years of Marie de Guise's regency. Undaunted, Mary set her staff and servants to work. The beds were richly coloured and embroidered

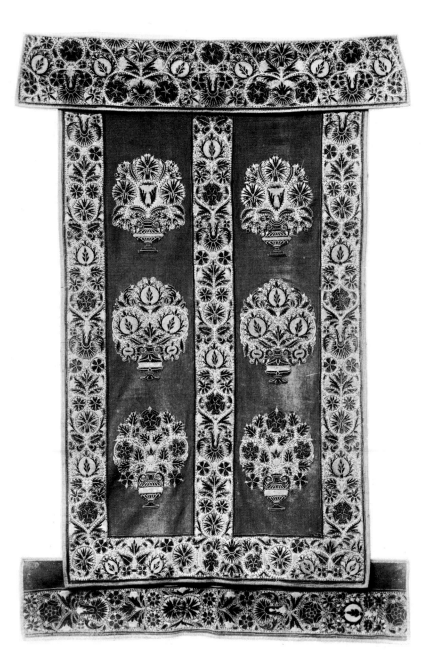

Plate 18
Red woollen hanging with remains of an upper and lower valance, with applied black silk embroidered in yellow silk with touches of blue. Said to have come from Lochleven castle where Mary was held prisoner June 1567– May 1568. (Trustees of the Royal Museum of Scotland.)

with gold and silver, some topped with 'stands of feathers'. Four such 'stands of feathers for the tops of beds' were listed in Edinburgh Castle in 1578. There were equally rich hangings on the walls and cushions on the seats, and Mary herself received courtiers and ambassadors sitting on a high chair against an embroidered hanging topped by a canopy edged on three sides with valances, or, as the Scots tersely described it, 'a false roof with three pands and a tail'.

Even in the Highlands, Mary's nobles lived in an unexpected degree of comfort considering the turbulence of their lives. After the rebellion of the Earl of Huntly and his son in 1562, his possessions were commandeered by the Queen and shipped to Edinburgh from Aberdeen. The indefatigable Servais de Condé noted among the movables eight beds, all of rich materials trimmed with gold and silver, with canopies and curtains. One, of yellow damask 'made like a chapel', was altered later and 'maid foure nukit' (into a four poster). Sir Colin Campbell of Glenorchy in Perthshire, who carried on constant war with his neighbours, especially the Clan McGregor, married his second wife Katherine Ruthven in 1550. They had embroidered hangings and beds in their castles of Finlarig and Balloch on Loch Tay. One set of valances embroidered in silk and wool upon canvas, bearing their arms and initials, still survives in the Burrell Collection, Glasgow, and is decorated with lively figures of Adam and Eve, a suitable choice for a couple who founded a large and flourishing family.

Another piece of the same period, probably a table carpet judging from the inscriptions on it, bears the arms and initials of Katherine Oliphant, a widow who married her second husband, George Dundas of Arniston, in 1565, the year in which Mary married Darnley. The table carpet has two medallions illustrating scriptural texts. One shows a gentleman, wearing a flat cap and voluminous coat, giving two loaves to a young beggar, apparently a cripple with a stick. Around is written *THE LORD COMANDES THE TO BREAK BREAD AND GYE YT YE HOUNGRY*. Above the elephant, a play on the name Oliphant, and the arms and initials K O for Katherine Oliphant, is another medallion. In it an elderly St. Paul, with beard and scanty hair offers a glass of wine to Timothy, wrapped up in a cloak and wearing a cap with ear flaps. Around it is the caption *PAUL SAYING TO TEMOTHE THK A LYTL VYN TO COMFORT THY STOMAK*. There is also a border of masks and fabulous monsters that has at some time been cut and patched with pieces from elsewhere. The carpet may at one time have been one of a matching pair.

Plate 19
Part of a panel or table carpet, with the initials K O for Katherine Oliphant, who married George Dundas of Arniston in 1565. St. Paul offers a glass of wine to Timothy (1 Timothy V.23). (Miss Dundas of Arniston.)

These textile furnishings suggest that there were professional embroiderers attached not only to the court, but who were available to undertake the drawing out and working of designs for anyone who could afford to pay for them. It is not clear whether there were professional workshops in cities such as Edinburgh, Perth and Aberdeen, or whether these professional embroiderers travelled from place to place. The designs may indeed have been drawn directly on to the stretched canvas or linen by travelling artists, who were not above decorating the walls or ceilings, as well as executing portraits of the family, whilst working in the country houses and castles. Certainly the Arniston table carpet and the Campbell valances have been drawn out by skilled draughtsmen, and then worked by amateur embroiderers, probably the ladies whose initials appear on the respective pieces, aided no doubt by members of their households.

Plate 20
Upper valance for a bed. The scene shows Daniel (centre) being raised from the lions' den on the order of the king (right). At the back (left) those who denounced him are being seized by the king's soldiers, and (below) being devoured by lions. On either side, ladies and gentlemen of the court watch. (Daniel VI, 23–4). (The Duke of Buccleuch and Queensbury.)

However the large number of fine sets of valances from castles and houses, mainly in the centre of Scotland, especially from Perthshire, do suggest a professional workshop of great competence. These valances worked in tent stitch in worsted show figures in French costume, and depict scenes from the Old Testament or the classics in the manner of a strip cartoon, often difficult to identify or disentangle. Because of the costume they have inevitably become associated with Mary Queen of Scots, although some of the costume details show fashions more typical of the subsequent reigns of Charles IX of France or his younger brother, Henry III. Clearly the Queen could not have worked all these valances herself, but it is often suggested that they were made by her embroiderers and that she presented them as gifts. Only one bed in the inventory of 1561 was of worsted – the 'auld bed' with satyrs and foliage – all the others, including those given as wedding presents by the Queen, were of silk and velvet. Two pounds of coloured worsted was issued on March 12th, 1561, to be given, not to the queen's embroiderers, but to the *tapissier* Pierre Martin, 'to amend the Queen's Graces tapestry'.

It would seem that the tent stitch valances were produced in workshops by professional embroiderers after Mary left Scotland. Some of them belonged to families who were attached to Mary's son James, who had his own court embroiderer, William Beaton. Mary's embroiderer, Ninian Miller, was still working in Edinburgh in 1583, and practised his craft as Freeman and Guild-brother of the City, which entitled him to his own workshop. There is no record of Pierre Oudry, who is thought to have followed his mistress to England.

The people of Scotland now worshipped in churches that were stark and bare, stripped of plate and vestments. In Edinburgh the provost, baillies (magistrates) and Burgh Council took over the vestments and plate of the Kirk of St. Giles to prevent their being spirited away, as they had been in Aberdeen. They were then held in safe-keeping until there was urgent need of cash to pay the stipend of John Knox. In 1561 it was decided to dispose of them 'to the maist advantage' in order to give 'John Knox, minister, the sum of fifty pounds for his quarter's payment'.

Before her return to Scotland Mary had been promised freedom to practise her own religion, and she and those of her courtiers who were Catholic heard Mass both at Holyrood and Stirling. Surprisingly Mary appears to have brought with her only one set of chapel furnishings: a crimson dossal and frontal embroidered with a crucifix and the queen's arms, powdered with gold stars, and a chasuble, stole and corporal case to match. The vestments at the Chapel Royal at Stirling comprised eleven copes, three of cloth of gold, and two old ones of blue damask powdered with gold fleurs-de-lys, with 'histories' on the orphreys. There were four High Mass sets of chasuble with two tunicles, two of which were cloth of gold, as well as two mourning sets of black velvet. There were also two altar frontals, one 'paned' cloth of gold with red silk, the other a black-velvet mourning frontal and pendicle.

The belongings of the rebel Earl of Huntly impounded by the Queen in 1562 included copes, chasubles and other vestments from Aberdeen Cathedral given to the earl for safe-keeping by the Catholic clergy at the time of the Reformation in 1560. Some of this rich collection of over fifty items appears to have been sets of vestments, copes, chasubles and tunicles, in cloth of gold or blue, green or red velvet. There is no note of their subsequent use in the Chapel Royal. On the contrary many were put to secular use. Servais de Condé noted: 'In March 1567, I delivered three of the fairest which the Queen gave to Lord Bothwell. And more (had taken) for herself a cope, chasuble and four tunicles to make a bed for the King (Darnley). All broken (up) and cut in her own presence.' Against the green velvet set is the note: 'In 1564 all this was employed by the Queen's command.' In the spring of 1565 he wrote: 'Three copes, two tunicles and a chasuble, all of green velvet, whose ornaments were broken up to decorate a bed with embroidery and flowers . . .' and sufficient was left over to cover a high chair, two seats and a *chaise percée* (commode).

Apparently the Queen never used her needle in the service of the Church, although an exceptionally beautiful set of chasuble, dalmatic and tunicle with two stoles, preserved at Blairs College, Aberdeen, is attributed to her. Worked on white satin, the chasuble has silver scrolling stems with flowers, such as lilies, roses, carnations and blue periwinkles, worked in coloured silks. The cross-shaped orphrey on the back has a rich design of vines worked in silks

52

with the letters IHS surmounted by a monstrance-like cross, all upon a laid ground of silver thread couched in circular whorls. The orphreys of dalmatic and tunicle have been worked to match in slightly heavier silk. These latter two vestments are made, not of embroidered satin like the chasuble, but of woven silk brocade on a white ground. There are two matching stoles. The dalmatic and tunicle appear to have been made up later in order to convert the sumptuous chasuble into a set suitable for High Mass.

It seems improbable that this very handsome and elaborate set was worked by Mary herself. The unusual pattern of the silver ground of the orphrey has so far been found only on pieces of German origin. Part of an altar frontal in the Marienkirche at Lübeck has gold thread laid in these circular whorls, and is believed to have been worked in south Germany. A chasuble in the cathedral of Frankfurt-am-Main has a similar ground and bears the arms of the Counts of Thurn and Taxis. Yet another vestment with this type of laidwork is illustrated by Louis de Farcy in his monumental book on French needlework. He rejects the idea of this piece having been made in France and firmly suggests a south German origin. It would appear, therefore, that though the design of the Blairs chasuble may be French, it is much more likely that the orphrey could have been made in south Germany. Although the set is traditionally believed to have come, like so many of the other treasures preserved at Blairs, from the Scots College in Paris, suppressed at the Revolution, and may therefore have been commissioned by Mary, there is a possibility that it might instead, like the silver-gilt mitre also at Blairs, have come from the Scots Benedictine monastery of St. James at Ratisbon founded about 1110. Until further evidence of its origin is forthcoming, this beautiful richly embroidered set must remain a tantalising enigma.

8 Little flowers on canvas

Against the background of the newly furnished royal castles of Scotland the Queen, young, vivacious and beautiful, brought the elegance and colour of France in her dress. Her personal wardrobe, as listed by Servais de Condé, is textile poetry, glowing with colour, glistening with gold and silver, encrusted with embroidery. The gaiety of the silks, damasks and velvets with their rich trimmings give an impression of the Queen very different from the grave figure in white and black that can be seen in her surviving portraits.

In 1561, as well as the royal robe of violet velvet, worn probably at the coronation of Francis II in Paris, she brought with her thirty-nine robes, richly embroidered, many of gold tissue, together with nineteen black robes. There were thirteen farthingales or skirts of cloth of gold, twenty-two others embroidered with or made of silk, as well as decorated underskirts and cloaks. Her jewels included not only the crown jewels of Scotland – she had handed back the crown jewels of France on the death of Francis II – but also a rich collection of personal jewels, pearls, gold collars, rings, ear-rings, bracelets and chains, some given her by Henry II and Francis II.

During the following five years many of the gowns were given away to one or other of her ladies or cut up to decorate yet another bed. The dresses of such costly material were nevertheless constantly being renovated, although new ones were also being made to the latest fashion. Servais de Condé went to Paris for three months from December 1564 to March 1565, presumably to make purchases, and the Queen herself sent to Paris for the latest fashion in gloves and other accessories.

Ten years after Mary's departure from Scotland a list was made of the remains of this wardrobe, still packed in trunks in Edinburgh Castle, after garments had been grudgingly sent to Lochleven, and others as grudgingly sent to her in England. No doubt people had taken their pick of the wardrobe as they had of her jewels, but the wardrobe was still impressive. There were forty-one gowns: one of yellow satin, furred and braided with silver; another 'of white and red figured velvet, high-necked, side-sleeved (? slit), the bodice cut out upon green velvet braided with silver'. Among the twenty-one farthingales was one in blue satin embroidered with gold and silver, and another was 'aurange satin' trimmed with silver. There were sixteen skirts, one of silver netting with carnation silk, and forty-five pairs of sleeves elegantly and richly embroidered, in purple, white, yellow and grey satin; or fine linen embroidered with gold, silver and black silk, or blue or crimson silk. Among the bed linen there were 'four English sarks (shifts for day or night wear) with blackwork' and 'An English sark of whitework'. There was 'a little hat of black taffeta embroidered all over with gold, with a black feather and gold, in a case', and 'another little gray felt hat embroidered with gold and red silk with a feather of red and yellow, in a case', as well as another of black taffeta embroidered with silver, two velvet bonnets, two old hats, one of 'aurange velvot' embroidered with silver, and one of white 'crisp' (gauze).

Hoods, coifs, collars and wrist frills, six pairs of velvet shoes, ten pairs of hose of gold, silver and silk, six pairs of gloves and three pairs of hose of Guernsey worsted complete the wardrobe. The last item reminds us sharply that most of the costumes, although heavy with golden braid and the necessary buckram stiffening, seem to have offered very little real warmth against the Scottish climate, when worn over shifts of fine linen. There is no mention of garments of Florence serge, only three 'hieland mantills', one blue, one white and one of black frieze, to offer some protection against the Edinburgh winds, and 'a nycht gowne of white boutclaith' (woollen cloth used for sieves) braided with white silk to wear as a dressing gown. The Queen had brought with her a dozen neck furs of ermine and sable, but these were listed among her jewels, because they had gold or jewelled heads and feet.

The queen's wardrobe was much larger than this when she first had to beg that clothes be sent for her to Lochleven, but what Servais de Condé was allowed to dispatch was embarrassingly meagre, as his list shows. This list, found among the papers of the Scots College in Paris, and first published by the Maitland Club of Glasgow in 1834, deserves careful attention. Servais de Condé does not appear to have been allowed to communicate directly with his mistress, so he made the list, no doubt intending to present it for her usual signature when she returned to Holyroodhouse. It would be proof that, although she had asked for more, he had sent all that was allowed. It is also important to note that the sewing materials, carefully listed as having been sent, were totally insufficient to complete the large hangings or valances of woollen tent stitch upon canvas that are now attributed to Mary during her imprisonment on Lochleven.

The list is headed in French 'Memorandum of all that I took from the coffers in the chamber, during the time that the Queen was at Lochleven and since, commencing July 1567'. But first, there was the silver basin and ewer sent with a little box and pins to Borthwick Castle, at which Mary had spent one of her last days of freedom with Bothwell. Then, 'in the same month of June I sent to Lochleven' a red satin skirt striped with white and furred with marten, a pair of black velvet boots also furred, a bodice of crimson satin, a holland cloak and bodice, quilted, black silk hose (*chausses*), pins, two pairs of shoes and a box of preserves.

In July de Condé sent two pairs of white serge hose or breeches and another pair in red woollen cloth, three pairs of shoes (two of black velvet, the other leather), a chemise and two bodice fronts, a little casket covered in crimson with F in silver-gilt. Also included were a dozen skeins of black silk, six of 'twisted Spanish silk' with silk in other shades (presumably the Spanish silk was also black) and another packet of smooth silks of all colours and shades. As well, there were the dozen and a half little flowers painted on canvas, and outlined in black silk.

In August more preserves and pins were sent. The vast quantity of pins was required to keep clothing in place, especially the stiff head-dresses and veils. Fine linen was sent to make underwear for the Queen, four collars gathered into ruffs, two pairs of sleeves, two bodices, handkerchiefs embroidered with gold or silk, more soap for washing her hands and a little box of scented powder. De Condé also sent a dozen skeins of black silk, on another occasion a packet of Spanish silk of all colours, four skeins of gold thread and four of silver.

On September 3rd the Queen wrote angrily for more clothing: 'ane doublet and skirt of white satin, ane aither . . . incarnat and blak and the skirts with thame . . . togither with the cameraige (cambric) and lynyn claith whereof I gave you a memorial, and if the schone (shoes) be not reddy made . . . send thame with some other eftir. Cause Servais to send two pair sheets . . . all the dry damas plums that he has, togither with the pens he has . . . ye shall cause make one dozen rasene nedillis (*réseau* needles = netting needles) and mowlis (*moulles* = gauges or mesh sticks); and speir at Servais if he has ony aither covering of beddis to me nor (except) green and send me to put under the tother covering.'

The clothing appears to have been sent. Certainly 'doublets' of crimson, black and white satin were sent in September, as well as six pairs of linen sheets, more collars and cuffs and yet more pins. The supply of preserved plums must have been finished, and there is no evidence that the pens or bed covering that the Queen demanded were ever sent.

It was not until October that Servais de Condé managed to send not only the netting needles and gauges requested, but also several of the queen's perukes or hair-pieces, together with two more bodices, sleeves, ruffs and head-dress.

In November a little alarm clock was sent, more pins, more linen for drawers for the Queen and handkerchiefs, but no more silks or canvas. Indeed the list for this period ends tersely:

During the month of December, Nothing.

In April I handed over six handkerchiefs worked and enriched with gold silver and silk.

-I handed over the said six handkerchiefs following the order of Mons[r] de Morra (the Earl of Moray) on the 27th April 1568.

Mary Seton, when she was allowed to join her, must surely have taken more clothes, but the only evidence of the garments finally assembled for Mary to wear during her ten months' captivity on Lochleven is to be found in the small list made on May 5th, 1568, three days after her escape. This was made by 'the Queen's Grace's master cook and Elles Boug his spous at Lochlevin'. They packed the clothes 'in a coffer', which was signed for by one of the queen's French servants on arrival at Edinburgh. There were five silk gowns, two others (presumably of wool since the material is not specified), three waistcoats or petticoats, a pair of sheets, eight sarks, two napkins and a kerchief, a pair of drawers (*calsons*) two or three pairs of hose, and 'ane saiting patecleyth' (a satin head-dress). Perhaps her women, allowed to leave after the queen's escape, took the rest.

Mary was not allowed the embroiderer she had asked for. It is clear from the list made by Servais de Condé that, unless she obtained wools and canvas from some other source, which seems unlikely, her needlework on Lochleven consisted of embroidery in silks – the little flowers on canvas sent in July. Flowers prepared in this manner for working, and never completed, are still to be seen at Traquair House, Peeblesshire, a house that Mary visited with Darnley.

Plate 23
Flowers, drawn on linen canvas and outlined in black silk, prepared for working. (Mr. Peter Maxwell Stuart of Traquair.)

Linen was sent for the queen's underwear, and the amount of black silk leads one to suppose that it was used for the fashionable blackwork that even the staid Earl of Moray did not disdain to wear on his shirt.

The netting needles and gauges may have been needed to make cauls or nets for the hair, especially if the Queen were wearing false hair while she was taking exercise on that small, windy island. Mary had been accustomed to wearing decorative nets over her hair while in France and cauls or snoods, sometimes decorated with pearls or gold, had been fashioned in netting since the Middle Ages. In the Germanisches Nationalmuseum, Nuremberg, there is a fine hairnet of blond knotted silk, darned with white silk and decorated with dice of green silk chain stitch. It was found in a medieval grave at Marburg, Hessen. Another medieval hairnet, even more elaborate, is in Düsseldorf. It is made of silk shields bearing heraldic motifs.

On the other hand it may be that the netting was made into squares of *lacis* with the intention of joining them together for a bed hanging or even for a dress. 'Eight small pieces of *réseuil* of white silk, begun to sew on and not perfect' were listed at Edinburgh Castle in 1578, as well as a long gown in the same technique, together with five 'little veils' of linen net, one large, two of them trimmed with pearl and black silk.

The little flowers on canvas, intended for application on to a larger piece such as a bed hanging, and the squares of *lacis,* are a reminder that in 1566, just before the birth of James and in preparation for the very real perils of childbirth at that time, Mary had made a will bequeathing her jewels in the event of the death of herself and the child. To Darnley she left 'the ring with which he married me'; her French relations were remembered, and her godson, Francis Stewart, was to receive the set of enamelled black and white buttons with the crescent symbol of Henry II of France and Diane de Poitiers that Mary had worn as a little girl. There are several *brodures* mentioned in the will, sometimes mistakenly described as embroideries, but they are all enamelled or jewelled.

Plate 24. Part of a bed hanging of crimson-brown velvet, with applied flowers worked in silk on canvas. (The Earl of Mansfield.)

The word, sometimes spelt *bordures,* is translated by Cotgrave in his *Dictionarie of the French and English Tongues,* published in 1611, as 'a border, welt, hem or gard of a garment'. It may well refer in this case not to the borders of dresses, but to the borders of head-dresses, like the one that Madame de Canaples wears in her portrait.

At the end of this will Mary added: '*Tous mes ouvrages masches et collets aux quatres Maries, a Jene Stuart, a Marie Asquin, Sonderland et a toutes les filles*'. ('All my net (mesh) work and applied work to the four Maries, Jean Stuart,

Marie Erskine, Sunderland, and to all my women.') On Lochleven, Mary was adding to the collection of her 'ouvrages masches et collets'.

It is not known what happened to the flowers that the Queen worked on Lochleven. They are not listed with the other belongings at Edinburgh Castle

Plate 25
Detail of the hanging.

in 1578. A set of bed hangings at Scone Palace are attributed to Mary and would fit this description, although there are considerably more than eighteen 'little flowers' worked on fine canvas in coloured silks.

Such decorations were easier to apply if a thin material, such as silk or fine linen, was pasted to the back before cutting out. It appears to have been done in this case. They are applied to a velvet which would be described in contemporary records as 'crimson-brown' and outlined in gold thread. At some time these hangings were altered to fit a different bed, but they were in constant use until a few years ago. As well as flowers there are insects, and a monkey and a small dog. Mary's fondness for little dogs is well known, and she was to embroider other dogs later. There is also a border made up of a twisted cord design, a common renaissance ornament. Inevitably this is read as M S, the initials of Mary Stuart, although they are also, of course, those of Mary Seton. Possibly this familiar border design was chosen because of its suggestion of the initials of both Marys. A more assured version of the same design is preserved at Hardwick Hall mounted on green velvet.

Many large pieces are attributed to Mary at this period: valances and hangings, and the red hangings from Lochleven now in the Royal Scottish Museum. However these would have required a frame several feet long, and each would have taken many months to complete. It is thus inconceivable that Mary could have executed even one, far less the number claimed to have been worked by her during the ten and a half months she spent on the island. They would also have required large amounts of canvas and worsted, and it is significant that only silks and metal thread in small amounts were sent to Mary on Lochleven. Indeed at no time in her life, apart from the time she was learning 'works' in her childhood, is there any record of her using anything but silk. We must accept, therefore, that she spent her time on Lochleven working on small pieces with whatever silks she could obtain, impatiently awaiting rescue or escape from her captivity.

ENGLAND

9 The Daughter of Debate

The sail in the fishing boat took four hours, but there is no record of Mary weeping at this last glimpse of her kingdom, as she had done when she left France. She felt certain that once she met Elizabeth, who had been so shocked by her imprisonment on Lochleven, she would receive help to return to Scotland and punish her rebellious lords. If she got no help from Elizabeth, then she must turn to France or even to Spain.

For Elizabeth and her advisers the sudden unannounced arrival of the Queen of Scots in England was an embarrassment. Mary had, after all, been accused by many of her people of taking part in the murder of her husband and marrying the chief suspect. She was a Catholic, and when Queen of France had had the temerity to style herself Queen of England. On the other hand she had entered England of her own free will, begging support and succour from her cousin, another female monarch, whose lawful successor she undoubtedly was.

Elizabeth could not sanction the raising of an army to support Mary against the Protestant lords of Scotland who had defeated her, nor could she allow her to travel to France, where Charles IX would welcome the chance of aiding his Catholic sister-in-law. She was equally determined not to receive Mary at court, where she would be entitled to a position next to Elizabeth herself, as a crowned queen and her nearest heir. There began therefore the long weary years of captivity for Mary in England, during which she was treated as a Queen and allowed her ladies and attendants, her chair of estate and her ambassadors to the English and French courts, but with her freedom rigidly curtailed, her correspondence strictly censored and the number of her attendants controlled. Mary was to develop all the subterfuges she had learned on Lochleven: the smuggling of letters, the wild promises, the appeal to likely and unlikely allies in her struggle to regain her freedom.

However, it was first necessary, as in Lochleven, to obtain clothes and money. The clothes were eventually sent, from London and from Edinburgh. Servais de Condé was obliged to add a sad footnote to the list begun the previous July of all the other requirements, small articles of dress and personal treasures, that he was permitted to send at various times to the Queen of Scots now she was in England, first to Carlisle and later to Bolton Castle. There was a net coif with gold thread, a packet of silk cord to make another, with eight packets of ribbons and gold thread. There were also eighty buttons of pearl, twelve pairs of ear-rings, a dozen embroidered handkerchiefs, six chemises decorated with blackwork, seven pairs of linen sheets, six pairs of silk garters, six dozen skeins of silk in black and other colours, fifteen pairs of hose in a variety of cut and colours, with nine of white crêpe. Pairs of sleeves were sent to enliven the queen's wardrobe, one pair made of black satin embroidered with *cannetille d'argent* (silver wire twisted into a spring-like shape) and another pair of silver net decorated with black silk bows.

In December 1568 de Condé despatched a gold pendant enamelled in black and white with some perfumed gloves and a clock: not the alarm clock that had been sent to Lochleven, but a little striking clock in a silver network bag.

Mary was joined by the faithful Mary Seton, who was skilful at dressing her hair and arranging her wigs, for the Queen in her headlong escape had cut off her hair in order to avoid being recognised. Like Queen Elizabeth she had a collection of these fashionable hair-pieces. In Carlisle, where she stayed while Elizabeth decided what to do about her unwelcome guest, Mary was lent horses, but these were hastily withdrawn when it was seen how skilful a rider she was, and how easy it would be for her to escape north.

She was persuaded – she had little choice – to move further south to Bolton Castle in Yorkshire, professing herself still to be the guest, not the prisoner, of Elizabeth. While she was there, a trial was arranged at York and at Westminster to examine the charges against her of complicity in her husband's murder. The evidence offered by Moray against the Queen, who did not appear, were letters said to have been written by Mary to Bothwell, found in a silver casket decorated with the letter F and a crown – the notorious Casket Letters, which have long since disappeared. They seem to have been treated with scepticism even at the trial, which was inconclusive. Mary's captivity continued. At the beginning of 1569 she was placed in the charge of George Talbot, sixth Earl of Shrewsbury, a wealthy nobleman with houses and estates in the centre of England and a Protestant, although he had many Catholic relations. His chief virtue as custodian of the Scottish Queen was his unquestioned loyalty to Elizabeth. He had married as his second wife Elizabeth (Bess Hardwick) who had already been married three times. By her second husband, Sir William Cavendish of Chatsworth, she had had eight children, and insisted on the marriage of her daughter Mary to Shrewsbury's son and heir Gilbert, and of her son Henry to his daughter Grace. By this means she kept the money and estates she had amassed by her various marriages in the family.

Bess, who had a masculine flair for business and money matters, was a compulsive builder. She rebuilt Chatsworth, her Cavendish home, and before she died at the remarkable age of 87, had built and furnished a new house at Hardwick, her ancestral home, which still stands, on top of a hill, with her initials E S in stone proudly flaunted against the sky.

Mary was first lodged at Tutbury Castle, one of the Shrewsbury residences, a gaunt draughty edifice for which furniture and hangings had to be hastily brought from Sheffield Castle, Shrewsbury's principal home. In spite of the discomfort, of which she complained bitterly in her letters, Mary was prepared to be gracious to her new jailer and his wife. Bess was herself a notable needlewoman. She was then rebuilding and furnishing Chatsworth, and although she was twenty years older than the Queen, no doubt she used the arrival of this distinguished captive to glean ideas for the decoration of her new house. Bess, the daughter of a small country squire, little more than a farmer, had by her exertions and advantageous marriages become a great lady. She was astute enough to realise that the Queen of Scots, who had also been Queen of France, had been accustomed to furnishings of an elegance and splendour greater even than those of the English court. Together they sat, as Bess's husband complacently noted, 'devising works', Bess with an eye to the furnishing of one of her houses, Mary to pass the time while her brain was busy planning her release, composing letters full of pleading and affection to Queen Elizabeth or angry uncensored ones to be smuggled to France, to the Pope or to Spain.

Shrewsbury noted in a letter to William Cecil, Elizabeth's Secretary of State, in March 1569, after Mary had been in his custody for three months: 'This Queen continueth daily to resort to my wife's chamber where with the Lady Lewiston (Livingston) and Mrs. (Mary) Seton she useth to sit working with the needle in which she much delighteth and in devising works.' A month before, a young man, Nicholas White, one of Elizabeth's envoys on his way to Ireland, had called at Tutbury to report on the prisoner. He found she had 'an alluring grace, a pretty Scotch accent, and a searching wit, clouded with mildness'. Her hair, he noted 'was all black and yet Mrs. Knollys told me that she wears her hair of sundry colours'. The Queen received the young man graciously, sitting under her cloth of estate. 'I asked her Grace, since the weather had cut off all exercise abroad, how she passed the time within. She said that all the day she wrought with her needle, and that the diversity of the colours made the work seem less tedious, and continued till very pain did make her to give over; and with that she laid her hand upon her left side and complained of an old grief newly increased there. Upon this occasion she entered on a pretty disputable comparison between carving, painting and work with the needle, affirming painting in her own opinion for the most considerable quality.'

The cloth of estate under which she sat to receive him bore the embroidered motto 'En Ma Fin Gît Ma Commencement' from Marie de Guise's impresa of the phoenix arising from the flames, '. . . which is a riddle I understand not', wrote White in his report. Mary had perhaps adopted it in memory of her beloved mother, but it is more probable that it was meant to remind those who saw it that in spite of her forced abdication, when she gained her freedom, she too would make a new beginning.

It was during these first years of her captivity in England that most of the surviving needlework that can be identified with Mary was worked. She and Bess were at first on good terms with each other, sharing a mutual interest in needlework, and Bess and her husband were still friendly, though later they became most bitterly estranged. Shrewsbury was understandably reassured when he saw his wife and his unpredictable captive sitting together 'devising works'. The search for designs involved leafing through books. The emblem books, as fashionable then in England as they had been in France, gave Mary many ideas for embroidery designs, with their Latin mottos conveying double meanings. Bess adopted some of the more obvious; others would no doubt have had to be explained to her, since her education in Latin and European languages had scarcely been as extensive as that of Mary. Indeed Bess appears to have led too active a life to have been a wide reader. At her death she did not leave a notable library among her vast possessions: merely a few religious books. The sources from which the designs were taken suggest that they were from the queen's books rather than Bess's, or at least that they came from books with which the Queen was familiar. The centrepiece of a square bearing the E S for Elizabeth Shrewsbury, with the motto 'Ingenii Largitor ('Bestower

of wit') is copied from an emblem in *Devises héroïques* by Claud Paradin, first published in Lyons in 1557. It illustrates the fable of the thirsty jackdaw, who, unable to reach water, filled a bowl with pebbles to raise the level until he could drink. It might be labelled instead 'Necessity is the mother of invention'. A long cushion, still at Hardwick, depicting Europa and the Bull, is drawn from the woodcut by Bernard Salomon, published at Lyons the same year, while Mary was Dauphiness of France, although the Hardwick design may have been copied from a later edition, since its border lacks the original's delicate fantasy and is framed instead in a rather heavy scroll (Plate 7).

The wonderfully clear woodcuts of birds, beasts and fishes by Conrad Gesner from the one-volume edition of 1560 offered a rich choice of needle-work designs, and must have caused endless discussion. Some were familiar creatures, like the jay and the capon, while others were exotic birds and animals, included by Gesner from various sources, such as the *Bird of Paradise,* whose legless skin, drawn as if laid out on a dissecting board, was faithfully copied on to canvas.

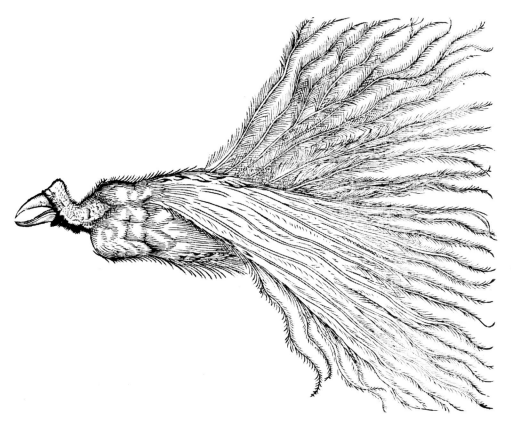

As well as Gesner's natural-history book Mary must have had access to that of Pierre Belon, since her panel of the leaping dolphin is taken from the wood-cut in his book published in Paris in 1551. It is more likely, however, that it was copied from a more popular little volume, *La Nature et Diversité des Poissons,* published in 1555, in which the same woodcut appears. This book has en-gaging short descriptions in French, which Mary and her women would enjoy reading and translating for Bess's benefit. One of the fabulous fishes, the *monk fish,* which appears also in Gesner with small variations, is copied instead from Belon. Beside it is a circumstantial description of these so-called sea monsters, with the dates of their sighting, much as the Loch Ness monster is nowadays recorded. Not only male *monk fish* had been known before, wrote Belon, but an observer in the Netherlands, Corneille Amsterdam, described a female sea monster, thrown up on to the Dutch coast during a great flood, and 'taken to the town of Edam, where she lived for some time with the women of the country, doing all the works and acts of a woman, except that she did not speak'.

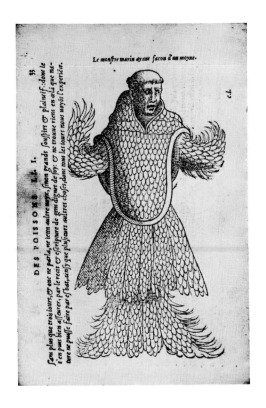

Plate 29
The Monkfish. P. Belon
La Nature et Diversité des Poissons, Paris 1555. (The National Library of Scotland, Edinburgh.)

Besides the little book of fishes Belon's beautifully illustrated book of birds *L'Histoire de la Nature des Oyseaux,* published in Paris the same year as the fish book, must have been read, for although many of the woodcuts in this volume are copied from Gesner, there are others used by Mary or Bess which do not appear in the Swiss work. These are the hobby, one of the birds used for hawking, a sport beloved of Mary, and labelled with its French name of *'hobreau',* as well as the *'fauconet'* and the *'robin'* on a hurdle.

The outlines of the creatures have been taken from the woodcuts, but their names have by no means been faithfully copied. Familiar birds and beasts are given their popular names – sometimes, when connected with hawking, in French. At other times the common English or Scottish name appears on the label. Thus the mole is a 'mold warpe', the kite is given the Scottish name common at that time a 'gleade', and the great snipe is labelled a 'pool snyte'. This last is still called a 'muir snite' in parts of Scotland. The spoonbill, errone-ously labelled *'pelicanus'* by Gesner, but given the correct German name of

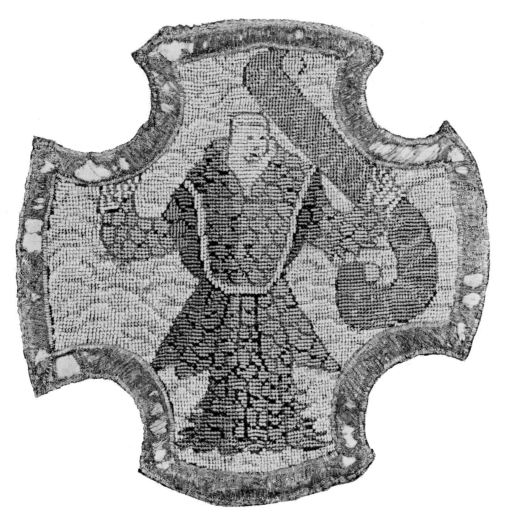

Plate 30
Panel. A SEA MOONKE.
(Victoria and Albert
Museum, Crown Copyright,
on loan to Oxburgh Hall.)

'loeffler', has been drawn out and identified with its common name 'a shofler', still called a 'shovelar' in parts of northern England.

Other panels still at Hardwick have been found by J. L. Nevinson to derive from illustrations in the works of an Italian botanist, Pietro Andrea Mattioli (1500–77), but whether these were worked at the time the Queen of Scots was in the custody of Shrewsbury has yet to be established.

Once chosen the design was drawn out on canvas by the embroiderer, who might also paint in the suggested colouring or work the outlines. Bess had her

Plate 31
Panel. THE HOBREAU.
(Victoria and Albert
Museum, Crown Copyright,
on loan to Oxburgh Hall.)

Plate 32
The Hobreau (The Hobby
Falcon) P. Belon *L'Histoire
de la Nature des Oyseaux*,
Paris 1555. (The University
of Edinburgh.)

68

Plate 33
Panel. SHOFLER
(Spoonbill). (Victoria and
Albert Museum, Crown
Copyright, on loan to
Oxburgh Hall.)

Plate 34
Pelicanus. C. Gesner *Icones
Animalium* 2nd Edition,
Zürich, 1560. (The University
of Edinburgh.)

Plate 35
**Panel. PHENIX with XR monogram. (Victoria and Albert Museum, Crown
Copyright, on loan to Oxburgh Hall.)**

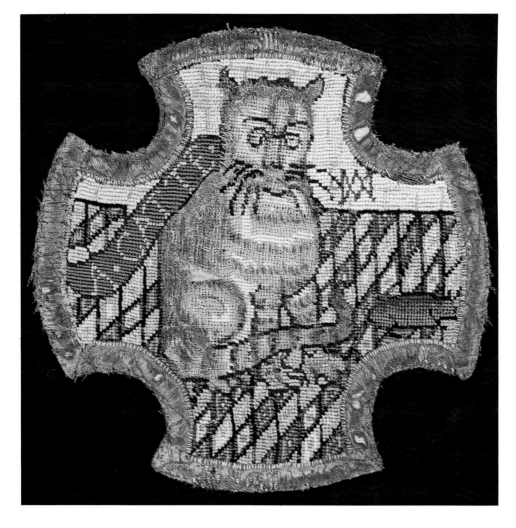

Plate 36
Panel. A CATTE from
the Oxburgh Hangings.
(Reproduced by
permission of the
Holyrood Amenity Trust.)
(See plate 43.)

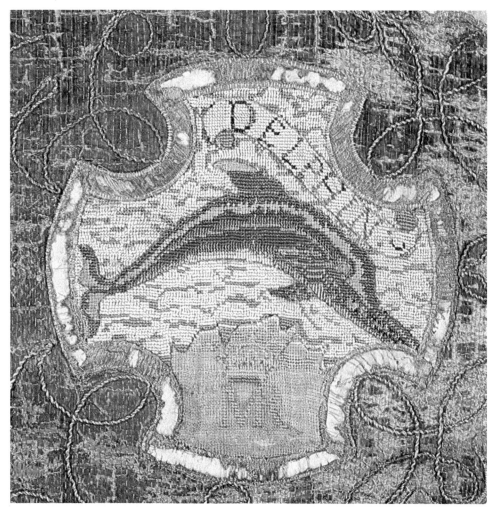

Plate 37
Panel. DELPHINE.
(Victoria and Albert
Museum, Crown
Copyright, on loan to
Oxburgh Hall.) (See
plate 44.)

Plate 38
Panel. POOLE SNYTE (The Great Snipe). (Victoria and Albert Museum, Crown Copyright, on loan to Oxburgh Hall.)

own embroiderer attached to her household. Although Mary's request for an embroiderer on Lochleven had been ignored, in England, where she was allowed thirty attendants (and usually she managed to have more) an embroider is mentioned several times, though not always by name. Pierre Oudry is thought to have joined her, as his name is on the portrait of Mary painted at Sheffield and now at Hardwick.

In most of the surviving embroideries of this period of the queen's life, the designs are drawn out with surprising fidelity to the original. Occasionally Gesner's woodcut is adapted, perhaps to accommodate a personal idea. The 'estriche', for instance, is copied from Gesner's luxuriantly plumed bird, but has a horseshoe in its mouth to illustrate the belief that it could digest iron. It was necessary for the embroiderer to be a skilled draughtsman, for the scale of the woodcut was often tiny compared with the spread of canvas required for the design. Bernard Salomon's woodcut of Europa and the Bull, for instance, measures a mere 53 mm. wide by 43 mm. deep. Even with exact squaring-up it is remarkable that so much of the original is recognisable in a panel measuring roughly a metre wide by half a metre deep.

It is understandable, therefore, that the discussion and choice of designs, the leafing through books that reminded her of France and the working of the panels of embroidery should offer welcome occupation to Mary, especially when 'the weather had cut off all exercises abroad'. Her life began to follow a tedious, frustrating pattern with needlework as occupational therapy. She wrote pleading letters to Elizabeth, begging to see her. She made all kinds of promises in exchange for her freedom. She wrote pathetic letters to her little

72

Plate 39
The Ostrich. C. Gesner
Icones Animalium 1560. (The
University of Edinburgh.)

Plate 40
Panel. THE ESTRICHE.
(Victoria and Albert
Museum, Crown Copyright,
on loan to Oxburgh Hall.)

son, hungry for news of him, but these were never answered. He was being brought up a Protestant, taught to believe that his mother was an adulteress and a murderess. She was denied a priest, but managed to get one as a rule in the official capacity of an attendant gentleman.

She used every means to increase the number of her small household. Shrewsbury scrutinised each member, and continually sought to reduce the number, since he found the cost of maintaining them and the necessary guards crippling. Elizabeth never allowed him enough money for the maintenance of the Queen of Scots. Mary wrote repeatedly to France for the revenue from her estates there, but her Guise relatives ignored her appeals. Her health deteriorated. She had constant pains in her side and severe headaches. She complained of the smells and the drains at Tutbury, and was moved to other Shrewsbury houses: to Wingfield Manor, then back to Tutbury; to Bess's new Chatsworth while Tutbury was 'sweetened', then to Sheffield Castle for nearly fourteen years. During her stay there she lived in the Lodge – a house in the park which had been specially strengthened in order to prevent her escape. While she was there, a few brief periods were spent at Buxton Spa, to which she went for treatment, and at Chatsworth (not the present building), and Worksop Manor, another Shrewsbury house.

But the tedium and frustration were punctuated by plans to escape and by secret messages delivered, in spite of Shrewsbury's vigilance, by those who got leave to visit her. In 1569 a marriage was suggested, which Mary seized upon as the means of escape. The Duke of Norfolk, a widower and a Protestant, who had presided over her trial at York, was approached by her ambassador to the English court, William Leslie, Bishop of Ross. Norfolk, a cousin of Elizabeth, was the only duke in England. He would, Mary felt, be acceptable to Queen Elizabeth. Norfolk's acceptance of the plan is less easy to understand. He was a man of great ambition, who lived like a prince on his estates in Norfolk, and was piqued that his claims to high office had been passed over by Queen Elizabeth in favour of men of inferior birth, such as Cecil and Robert Dudley, Earl of Leicester. Norfolk's third wife was the widow of Thomas, Lord Dacre of Gillsland in Cumberland. She was a devout Catholic, and Norfolk had seen the strength of Catholic feeling still burning in the north of England. It is possible that the plan to marry Mary was merely to ensure that, if anything happened to Elizabeth, as Mary's husband he would take his rightful place beside the throne. Norfolk had apparently never met Mary. Indeed, while president of her trial at York the previous year he had been persuaded that she had some hand in the death of Darnley. However, a secret correspondence began, Mary's letters becoming increasingly more tender as she persuaded herself that he was a little in love with her. Norfolk sent her a diamond ring, which she wore round her neck. The intrigue added a touch of hope and suppressed excitement to the weary round of her days.

The marriage plan leaked to the north of England, where it was regarded as a signal to the Catholics that the time had come to depose Elizabeth and rescue Mary in order to restore the Catholic religion. An army was gathered, and marched south. Elizabeth hastily ordered Mary to be moved to Coventry out of reach of the rebels. There she had to spend a night in an inn before a house could be found for her. But the rebels lacked leadership, the revolt disintegrated, and its wealthier members were given crushing fines. Norfolk, although he had made no attempt to join them, was imprisoned in the Tower of London. He was released in August 1570.

Mary had not given up hope, however, and almost immediately she and Norfolk became implicated in a new plot. The Pope had issued a bull, *Regnans in Excelsis*, excommunicating Elizabeth and absolving her Catholic subjects from loyalty to her. Mary thus became even more the hope of the Catholics, and she lent herself the more readily to a plan devised by an Italian, Ridolfi, by which she should marry Norfolk and succeed to the throne of England after Elizabeth had been deposed with foreign help. The plan was hare-brained, but Mary was willing to do anything to end her unjust and wearisome imprisonment.

In the meantime the needlework sessions with Bess continued. Part of the summer was spent at Chatsworth, the splendid mansion, by then nearly finished, built by Bess on the estate left to her by Sir William Cavendish. Bess embroidered a panel, probably a cushion for the new house, as a memorial to her late husband. The design, tears falling on to quicklime, and the motto 'Extinctam Lachrimae Testantur Vivere Flammam' ('Tears witness that the quenched flame lives') had been an *impresa* of Catherine de Medici, and must have been suggested by Mary as a suitable and fashionable memorial to express devotion to a dead husband, even though he had been succeeded by two more. In the border are other symbols of grief and mourning: a fan with falling feathers (a play on the word *penne*, plume and *peine*, grief); a glove, that symbol of fidelity, cut in two; broken interlaced cords; a cracked jewelled mirror; a snapped chain; and, to symbolise Bess's three previous widowhoods, three intertwined broken finger rings. As well as the Cavendish arms and motto 'Cavendo Tutus' ('By guarding safe') there was a twisted snake and a stag, both Cavendish symbols, and the initials W C and E C for William and Elizabeth Cavendish. The panel was dated 1570 and finished off with Bess's current initials, E S, under the coronet of a countess.

About the same time Mary was working another panel of roughly the same size. Like the panel worked by Bess its design was an emblem, a hand wielding a pruning hook, cutting the young unfruitful branches from a vine, with the motto 'Virescit Vulnere Virtus' ('Virtue flourishes by wounding'). It was within a trellis of flowers and fruit, and bore Mary's cipher ⊕ (the letters MA superimposed on the Greek letter Φ for Francis, her first husband, which was engraved on the inside of her signet ring) together with the royal arms of Scotland. It appeared to be a pious exercise on the part of the captive breathing the spirit of Christian resignation, but the panel was intended to convey a very different message. Mary sent it to Norfolk, and the message was plain for him to read: the unfruitful branch of the royal house (Elizabeth) was to be cut down; the fruitful branch (Mary) would be left to flourish and bear more fruit. When Ridolfi's plot was uncovered, Mary's ambassador, the Bishop of Ross, was imprisoned, and under threat of torture revealed that she had been in correspondence with Ridolfi, and had sent the cushion with its equivocal message to Norfolk.

Plate 41
Cavendish panel, with initials E S and symbols of mourning for Sir William Cavendish, second husband of Elizabeth, Countess of Shrewsbury ('Bess of Hardwick'). (Victoria and Albert Museum, Crown Copyright, on loan to Oxburgh Hall.)

Plate 42
Norfolk panel. A hand cutting down the unfruitful branches of the vine, with the motto
'Virescit Vulnere Virtus' ('Virtue flourisheth by wounding'), and Mary's cipher and the
royal arms of Scotland. (Victoria and Albert Museum, Crown Copyright, on loan to
Oxburgh Hall.)

Norfolk was tried, sentenced to death and executed in 1572. The English Parliament, alarmed by the threat to Elizabeth's life, clamoured for Mary's death also. The news of the massacre of the Huguenots in Paris on the eve of St. Bartholomew, a massacre instigated by Mary's relatives, the Guises, fanned the bitterness against Mary even more. Elizabeth, although pressed by Parliament and public opinion in London and the south of England, stood firm, and refused to countenance the execution of Mary. Instead Mary was deprived of her succession to the throne, and made liable to trial by peers of the realm if she plotted again against the Queen. Elizabeth wrote:

The daughter of debate, that eke discord doth sow,
Shall reap no gain where former rule hath taught still peace to grow.

Mary heard of the execution of Norfolk with grief; not perhaps so much for the death of a man she had probably never met as for the death of her plans for freedom. She continued to take an interest in Norfolk's orphaned children, who would have become her step-children. She took a special interest in Norfolk's eldest son, Philip, aged fourteen at the time of his father's death, who had contracted a childhood marriage with Ann Dacre, the eldest daughter of Norfolk's third wife by Lord Dacre of Gillsland. This was Norfolk's 'well-beloved Nann, that hath been as dear to me as if you had been mine own daughter', as he wrote in a poignant letter before his execution. He begged Ann to care for all his young children, as well as her own orphaned sisters, and Mary heard how steadfastly the fourteen-year-old girl had shouldered this charge. Like her mother Ann was a devout Catholic.

Later Mary heard with pain that Philip, after studying at Cambridge and before he had begun to live with his young wife, was attending the court, where Elizabeth preferred her younger courtiers unmarried. In order to gain favour of the Queen he cut himself off from Ann, and indeed was heard to question the validity of his marriage. When the story came to Mary's ears she devised a cryptic embroidery for Ann Dacre, just as she had for Norfolk. Worked in silks and silver it showed a tree on which sat two turtle doves. The right side of the tree had a few green leaves, but the left showed bare branches. Above was a motto 'Amoris Sorte Pares' ('Equals by the fortune of love'). Under the dove sitting on the leafy side was a motto in silver reading 'Hoc Ademptum' ('This has been taken away') with an anchor for hope, while under the dove on the bare branches was inscribed 'Illa Peremptum' ('There it has been destroyed') with pieces of broken boards to symbolise that Ann, while her husband still lived, had hope, but that Mary mourned without hope, since the Duke was dead. Ann's hope was realised: her husband became devoted to her.

In the meantime the needlework sessions with Bess still continued. The small panels bearing Mary's cipher might be chosen innocently enough from an emblem book or from Gesner's book of birds, beasts and fishes, but could be given a hidden meaning to those with eyes to see. Gesner's full-page woodcut of the domestic cat, for instance, could be embroidered as a ginger cat (Elizabeth's red hair was famous) wearing a small gold crown, regarding a small mouse, a detail not in Gesner's original. The leaping dolphin, a woodcut from Belon, bears the title *Delphin*, but those with a knowledge of French recognised the pun on the word *dauphin* for dolphin. The panel of the 'She

Plate 43
The Cat. C. Gesner *Icones Animalium* 1560. (The University of Edinburgh.)

Plate 44
The Dolphin. P. Belon *La Nature et Diversité des Poissons*, Paris 1555. (The National Library of Scotland, Edinburgh.)

79

Dolphin Fishe', perhaps intended as a companion, has been at some time cut in half and joined to another fish panel.

The panels bearing the initials E S for Elizabeth Shrewsbury were much less obscure. Small panels could be worked when sitting with the Queen, but Bess's overriding need was for large embroideries with which to embellish her houses, especially Chatsworth. Later she was to affirm that she 'never had but one imbroiderer at one time that worked on them' at Chatsworth, although he had been helped out by 'some of the Countess's grooms, women and some boys she kept'. The large appliqué hangings, now at Hardwick, one of which is dated 1573, showing female figures representing the Virtues, are composed of patchwork of brocade, velvet and gold tissue. They are professional work requiring a large frame, and the material appears to have come from vestments. Indeed Bess admitted that the 'imbroiderer' had used 'copes bought by Sir William St. Loe at Chatsworth'. Sir William had been Bess's third husband. Mary could advise as to the most effective use of these expensive materials, since she had used copes and other vestments in the furnishings of a bed for Darnley, and had given others to Bothwell for the same purpose.

Plate 45
Part of a hanging.
LUCRETIA, one of a set of
five hangings, each twelve
feet high, representing the
Virtues. Applied damask,
velvet and cloth of gold.
(The National Trust and the
Victoria and Albert
Museum, Crown Copyright.)

Plate 46
A detail of the hanging, showing the different materials applied.

Queen Elizabeth was constantly suspicious that Shrewsbury was succumbing to Mary's charms, even though he took great pains to emphasise that his relationship with her was solely that of custodian. Shrewsbury was always courteous to her, treating her with correct, if icy, civility, but she was constantly devising ways of evading his strict vigilance and trying to introduce messengers or messages through his tight security screen. The slightest relaxation of the rules brought down an irate message from Elizabeth. He was, therefore, mortified to discover in April 1574, that the Queen of Scots not only helped his wife to choose designs for the vast number of embroidered furnishings that were being prepared for Chatsworth, but that Bess was also getting the Queen to send to Paris for silks that could not be obtained in London. He wrote to the Secretary of State, Walsingham, in a fever of anxiety: 'Having received your letter by one Lyddell, a Scot, servant of this Queen

(Mary) and perceiving her Majesty's pleasure for his repair hither, I have searched and found all the tokens and other things which he brought, and will be careful of him while he stays. I found a note stating that Mons. Vergier, who attends to her dowry in France, has sent some silks for my wife (as she asked him while he was here) by a courier in London. For these my wife should pay this Queen about 160 crowns, but I, scrupulous in such matters touching her, will not deliver her any money till her Majesty (Elizabeth) is acquainted therewith.'

Three years later, on December 5th, 1577, Mary wrote to France from Sheffield asking for a bed of rich materials to be sent for the Shrewsburys, together with half a dozen 'grand chandeliers de sal(l)e' which were made at Crotelles, to be sent well packed. These gifts, which would be very acceptable to Bess, were no doubt meant, like those sent to Queen Elizabeth, to encourage some relaxation of her captivity. It would be interesting to know if they were ever sent, and if they were sent, whether they arrived.

Meanwhile Bess needed all the silks she could amass, for it was in this year that the large table carpet, now at Hardwick, was made with the central oval showing the Judgement of Paris, the date 1574 and the initials E S in a rich border of fruit and foliage, birds and animals. Mary also planned an ambitious piece. It was to be sent as a gift to Elizabeth, and she had written to the French ambassador in London: 'I must give you the trouble of acting for me in smaller matters, *viz.* to send me as soon as you can eight ells of crimson satin of the colour of the sample of silk which I send you, the best that can be found in London, but I should like to have it in fifteen days, and one pound of the thinner and double silver thread . . .'

It was a skirt, the crimson satin lined with taffeta of the same colour, completed in May and sent, beautifully packed, sealed with Mary's own seal. She wrote to the French ambassador asking him to present it on her behalf to the Queen 'as evidence of the honour I bear her, and the desire I have to employ myself in anything agreable to her'. Shrewsbury had his usual reservations about the gift, and wrote to Walsingham saying: 'Some in my house are infected with the measles, and it may be dangerous for the Queen to receive anything hence before it has been well aired. God long preserve her. She is a precious jewel to all men.'

A skirt that would fit this description, said to have been embroidered for Elizabeth by Mary while a prisoner, is in a private collection near Norwich. The needlework is of coloured silks with gold and silver threads, and shows a well drawn design incorporating honeysuckle, pinks, daffodils, lilies and roses. Surmounting each scrolled point is a thistle. It has descended to its present owner through the Lee-Waring family from William Dering, a page at the court of Charles I, Mary's grandson. The skirt has apparently been altered at some later date to convert into a hanging, possibly an altar frontal, as, indeed, happened to another of Elizabeth's skirts. The design is elegant and stylish, and if worked by Mary would seem to be a little in advance of contemporary English fashion.

Shrewsbury's anxieties did not prevent the gift from reaching Elizabeth and being accepted by her, for the French ambassador wrote to his King later

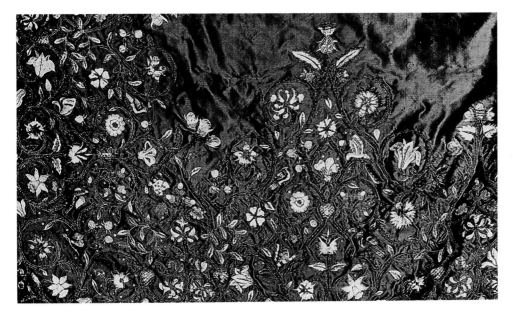

Plate 47
Part of a red satin skirt, embroidered in silk and metal thread, said to have been made for Queen Elizabeth by Mary Queen of Scots. (Mrs. Bulwer-Long.)

that month: 'The Queen of Scots, your sister-in-law, is very well, and yester-day I presented on her behalf a skirt of crimson satin, worked with silver, very fine and all worked with her own hand, to the Queen of England, to whom the present was very agreable, for she found it very nice and has prized it much; and she seemed to me that I found her much softened towards her. I have some letters of the said Queen, your sister-in-law, written to your Majesty, but I have not yet permission to send them to you.'

Elizabeth may have been pleased with a skirt, worked with French elegance, to add to her enormous wardrobe, but no easing of Mary's restrictions resulted. She was only occasionally permitted to ride – the exercise she had so much delighted in – and an increasing lameness made her beg for treatment in the baths at Buxton. She was only very occasionally allowed to go there for this purpose, even though Shrewsbury built a house made specially secure for her reception. Mary heard Mass by stealth, whenever a priest could be introduced disguised as one of her gentlemen. She wrote to the Archbishop of Glasgow in 1574 saying that her little flock were all Catholics, and asking if prayers in the vulgar tongue were permitted after they had said their Hours: 'It will be charity if you give the prisoners a rule. We have almost as much leisure as the inmates of a convent'. A little later she wrote again: 'As for myself, thank God, I still have sufficient remains of Latin to pray, more than of devotion; but I should like to observe the commands of the Church.' The same year on September 22nd she wrote asking him to beg her Cardinal uncle to send her a couple of pretty little dogs, 'for apart from reading and sewing, my only pleasure is in the small animals I can keep. Send them in baskets, warmly packed'.

With all other pleasures denied her it is understandable that her needlework became more and more important. As on Lochleven large pieces were im-practicable, because of the size of the frame required. In any case to embark on a large piece meant admitting to herself that a long period of time would be available for its completion. Mary was daily scheming for an escape from her captivity. A small piece of needlework, capable of being held in the hand, was not only convenient: its beginning and completion made the time pass more quickly. The cushion for Norfolk, the skirt for Elizabeth that took three

months to complete, were worked feverishly as presents for those who might end her imprisonment. She was not allowed to meet either, so she sent instead a very personal plea worked by herself.

The smaller pieces – the little flowers drawn on canvas, the birds and beasts and especially the emblems – were begun and finished as month succeeded month. Sometimes when Mary felt particularly well, she would work a small piece on fine canvas (36 threads to the inch) with emblems from the *Fables* of Gabriel Faerno, a new edition of which had been published in 1573 in Antwerp. She continued hopefully to make gifts for Elizabeth. As a New Year gift in

1575 she worked and sent her a piece of *lacis*. Like the satin skirt it was presented through the French ambassador, with many pretty compliments and the rather transparent request that her maid, Rallay, who had served her from her early days in France, be allowed a passport to go to France to bring back a girl to help her invent new patterns. Undeterred by the refusal, in the following March she sent Elizabeth three *coyfures de nuit* worked by herself. These would have been nightcaps or possibly head-dresses, not nightdresses as is usually stated.

There were constant arguments between Mary and Shrewsbury about the number of her household, nominally fixed at thirty persons. This included her Master of Household, Mary Seton, her women of the bedchamber, her secretary, pages, cook, laundresses, maids and scullions. There was a constant stream of messengers to and from London, Scotland and France, with Shrewsbury anxiously scrutinising each one's credentials, luggage and the letters they brought the Queen. Everything had to be reported to Elizabeth and the cost of the retinue constantly spiralled. Elizabeth, typically, kept him waiting for payment, and when it came, it was much less than requested. He suffered increasingly from gout, and finally became estranged from Bess.

They quarrelled, of course, about money. Bess's grandiose building and furnishing schemes for her own houses, not his, swallowed up vast sums. She accused him of improper relations with his prisoner. His life became almost unbearable, torn between three demanding, intelligent and unscrupulous women: his Queen, to whom he owed his allegiance; his captive, who believed herself unjustly imprisoned; and his rapacious wife, whose mind was set upon the splendour of her houses and her ambitions for her children.

10 The thread is cut

With only her needlework to comfort her and all too infrequent exercise it is not surprising that Mary's health deteriorated, and that she grew more introspective and depressed. She heard of the death of Bothwell in 1578. He had died insane, a prisoner in a Danish castle. Mary continued to write affectionate letters to her son, James, although these were rarely answered, even as he grew older, since he had his eyes firmly fixed on the English throne. She also sent him gifts. At Arundel Castle, Sussex, a set of child's reins are preserved, said to have been worked by Mary for her son. They consist of a heavily embroidered breast-piece, worked in gold and silver thread, with intertwined flowers: rose, pink, pomegranate and thistle, with a crowned sceptre and harp in the centre. The straps of red silk, now faded to a soft pink, edged with narrow gold fringe, are embroidered with the words *'Angelis Svis Devs Mandavit De Te Vt Cvstodiant Te In Omnibvs Viis Tvis'* ('God hath given his angels charge over thee: to keep thee in all thy ways'). Each word is separated by a sceptre, lion, swaddled infant, or heart, each surmounted by a crown.

If these are indeed the work of the Queen, made for her son while he was learning to walk, they must have been made during the early months of her captivity in England, since James was nearly two years old when she fled from Scotland. It would seem more probable that the reins were sent to Arundel, the home of Ann Dacre, after the birth of her daughter or that of her son, born after his father was imprisoned.

On September 15th, 1578, Mary wrote to France, sending the design of an emblem, which unfortunately she did not describe in her letter, asking for it to be made into a gold and enamel jewel to be sent to James by one or other of the gentlemen travelling from the French court to Scotland. About 1579 Mary devised a book for her son, *Tetrasticha, ou Quatrains à son fils,* writing out the verses and embroidering the cover. Whether James acknowledged this gift or not, after he had become King of England, Bishop Montagu of Winchester could write in 1616: 'The Quene his Majesties Mother wrote a book of verses in French of the Institution of a Prince, all with her own hand, wrought a cover of it with a needle, and is now of his Majestie esteemed as a precious jewel.' The book has since disappeared.

In 1583 Mary Seton, the only one of her four Maries who had remained unmarried and at her side, retired owing to ill health to spend her remaining days in the convent of St. Pierre at Reims, at which Mary's aunt was abbess.

Mary continued to take an interest in the children of the executed Norfolk, especially his daughter-in-law, Ann. Philip, her husband, had become a Catholic like his wife, a most dangerous step for a courtier and one so closely related to Elizabeth. Rather than return to court, in 1585 he decided to leave England and live quietly on the Continent, but he was caught escaping in a small fishing boat, and imprisoned with the utmost severity in the Tower of London. On the birth of his son a few months later, his captors, knowing how much he hoped for an heir, told him at first the child was a daughter. Ann was never allowed to see her husband again, though he lived on until 1595. He died, it is said, of eating a poisoned roast teal, and remained loyal to his wife's faith to the last.

It is possible that on hearing of his imprisonment Mary began a cushion that carried a message of sympathy and encouragement like the one she had sent earlier to his wife, although apparently she never got an opportunity to send it. In an inventory of her belongings made in 1586 there was 'a square of *petit point,* with a single emblem in the middle and others around [it] with the arms of France, Scotland, Spain and England'. A panel survives which would fit this description, and it would seem to refer to Philip Howard. Although mutilated, it shows an armillary sphere, from which feathers fall into a stormy sea filled with ships and sea-monsters, the sea from which Philip was taken to his imprisonment. The Spanish motto, *'Las Pennas Passan Y Queda La Speranza'* ('Sorrows pass but hope survives'), and the emblems with their mottos carefully arranged in the border all reinforce the message of fortitude and courage under crushing adversity. They come from many sources. Those immediately obvious are the hand cutting the Gordian knot, the viper coming out of the heat and fastened on a hand, with its Biblical quotation, *'Quis Contra Nos'* ('If God be for us, who can be against us?'), and hands clasped around a cornucopia, signifying a faithful servant.

All these emblems might be taken as referring to Mary herself, but if she had sent the cushion to Philip Howard, the arms of the four countries in each corner surrounded with the collar of their respective orders of chivalry would have carried their own significance, and would have been instantly understood. His father, the Duke of Norfolk, who, as Earl Marshal of England, had done so much to reorganise the College of Arms, had been a Knight of the Garter, which on this panel surrounds the arms of England. The Order of St. Michael, which surrounds the French arms, had also been conferred on Philip's father. In 1567, Elizabeth had sent the Order of the Garter to the young French King, Charles IX, and in return he had sent his ambassador to confer the Order of St. Michael on two of Elizabeth's most distinguished subjects, since she herself, being a woman, could not receive it. Her choices were Robert Dudley, Earl of Leicester and the Duke of Norfolk. Mary was aware of all this, for on the day following the ceremony the French ambassador travelled to Scotland to confer the same honour on her husband, Henry Darnley.

The Spanish arms surrounded by the collar of the Order of the Golden Fleece are inexplicable in any embroidery of Mary Stuart, because they could not refer to her. On the other hand Philip himself was not only named after Philip II of Spain as a result of his father's attendance on that monarch when

Plate 49
Panel. Once part of the
Oxburgh Hangings with an
armillary sphere and motto
*'Las Pennas Passan Y Queda
La Speranza'* ('Sorrows pass
but hope survives'), with the
arms of France, Spain,
England and Scotland.
(Victoria and Albert
Museum, Crown Copyright,
on loan to Oxburgh Hall.)

he had come to England in 1554 to marry Mary Tudor, but he was the godson of Philip, who had personally stood sponsor for him at his baptism.

The emblem below the French arms, a ribbon interlaced with columns below a crown and the motto *'Pietate Et Justitia'* was the device of Charles IX who conferred the Order of St. Michael on Norfolk. Although Mary's cipher is not evident on the panel, the royal arms of Scotland surrounded by the Order of the Thistle with her emblem above of the marigold turning towards the sun, and below, the dog, symbolising a faithful friend, would demonstrate clearly to Philip the identity of the sender of the cushion.

But it was never sent, for by the time Mary heard of Philip's incarceration her own imprisonment had become more severe. In September 1584, she had been removed, after more than fourteen years, from Shrewsbury's custody, and returned to the hated Tutbury Castle in the charge of Sir Amyas Paulet, a puritan and a martinet, who was ordered to keep her in strict confinement. She was not allowed out, and the Tutbury smells were worse than ever. She was moved to Chartley at Christmas 1585, a house surrounded by a moat, but her health scarcely improved until the summer.

Mary's correspondence was also being more strictly censored than ever, but she managed to smuggle letters out and to receive them by means of a brewer who supplied the house with beer. This correspondence was discovered by Walsingham, who intercepted and deciphered each letter before passing them on.

It was thus that she became implicated in the Babington Plot, a conspiracy of Catholic gentlemen, headed by a young man called Sir Anthony Babington, to assassinate Elizabeth and place Mary on the throne of England. Mary fell into the trap. Utterly cut off, ignored by her son James, who had no intention of encouraging his mother's release, she agreed to the scheme, even though it would mean 'the dispatch of the offending Competitor' (Elizabeth). Her letter of agreement was duly intercepted, the conspirators arrested and executed, and she herself taken in September 1586, to Fotheringhay Castle, a state prison. Here, on October 15th, she was tried in the great hall of the castle by judges and peers of England, including Shrewsbury. Mary answered her accusers with courage and dignity, denying their right to try her, the sovereign of another country, who had come to their land seeking assistance. When charged with plotting the death of Elizabeth, she denied it, although 'I do not deny that I have earnestly wished for liberty and done my utmost to procure it for myself. In this I acted from a very natural wish.' The following day Mary made a dignified and closely reasoned speech in her own defence. Her bearing at the trial, after years of captivity, no longer young and beautiful, but middle-aged, lame and ill, won her more respect and remembrance than any other event in her life.

Mary realised clearly how it would end. She was declared guilty by the Council, but Elizabeth still hesitated from signing the death warrant of a Queen. When she finally did so, the deed was carried out before she could change her mind. No protest came from Mary's son in Scotland, now twenty. Mary calmly made arrangements for her death, providing for her servants, relatives and friends. Ann Dacre, wife of Philip Howard, was to receive a book of prayers and the golden rosary Mary would carry to the scaffold.

On the day of her execution, February 8th, 1587, she was refused a Catholic chaplain. Two of her women were allowed to accompany her to the great hall, in which the block had been set up. Jane Kennedy helped her out of her black gown, below which she wore a red petticoat and red satin bodice. She put on a pair of red sleeves, and finally Jane Kennedy bound her eyes with a white cloth embroidered in gold. The axe fell, and the executioner held up her head with its auburn hair. Those who watched were horrified to see the head fall to the ground, for the auburn hair was a wig, and the scalp was covered with the short sparse grey hairs of a woman old before her time. As they gazed, from beneath her skirt crept her pet dog, who whined piteously beside the headless body. With this last, pathetic, faithful friend beside her, the Queen of Scots' captivity was ended.

11 The Chartley inventory

At Christmas 1585 Mary had been moved from the hated Tutbury to the moated manor-house, Chartley Hall, ostensibly on account of her failing health. It was here that she lived while the Babington Plot took shape. On June 13th, 1586, an inventory was made of all her belongings at the Hall, and a list of her servants was made with a view to seeing how many could be dismissed.

The inventory shows clearly the changed fortunes of the Queen. In place of the gaily coloured opulent clothes, some of which were no doubt still lying in trunks in Edinburgh Castle, the wardrobe listed is that of a middle-aged, ailing woman, who wore warm and sombre clothes. All except two of the fourteen gowns are black, one bordered with ermine, others trimmed with jet. Only one is of scarlet cloth, another is tawny Florence serge, the bodice trimmed with black velvet, with double sleeves, the outer sleeve long and straight the inner one of matching cut satin. There are more than a dozen cloaks, four of them furred, all black except for one of violet. There were three cloaks for night wear, presumably as dressing gowns, since the Queen would not have gone out at night. One was grey and furred, one white serge and another grey frieze (a thick woollen cloth). All other garments were either black or white, except for five petticoats: two crimson-brown, two carnation and one of scarlet trimmed with blue silk.

Many of these garments reappear in the list made after her death. They were carefully distributed according to the wishes of the Queen herself among the servants who had been permitted to stay to the end. Her maid, Renée Rallay, received the black velvet gown trimmed with ermine. Even so the list does not include the embroidery and needlework given into Rallay's safe keeping at Chartley on July 18th, 1566, except for a splendid embroidered bed, with upper and lower valances, embellished with gold and silver. This was apparently the 'furniture for a bed wrought with needlework, of silk, silver and gold, with divers devices and arms, not thoroughly finished' and was 'to be delivered to the King of Scottes'.

This bed, encrusted in emblems, was described in detail by William Drummond of Hawthornden in a letter to Ben Jonson in 1619, after it had been sent to England with three other beds 'to be mendit and providit with furnitour answerable and sutable to the beddis', in preparation for James's only visit to Scotland after 1603.

Apart from the bed the inventory taken at Chartley in the Queen's presence is of importance since it lists other pieces of needlework, many of them unfinished or unmounted:

A carnation satin table-cover worked in colours decorated with silver bullion, with three (unfinished) sides of a border, one ready to apply to it;

A square with yellow ground, powdered with white and red roses;

Another square with white ground, with flowers in compartments;

Another square, in strips of needlework and green velvet, powdered with silver stars;

Another square, made in tent stitch (*petit point*) with a single emblem in the centre and others around, the arms of France, Scotland, Spain and England in the corners (see Plate 49);

The story of Esther and Haman in a square;

Another square with red ground, not yet enriched, with roses and thistles in compartments . . . for a bed;

Two pieces of canvas, worked in compartments with silk in cross stitch, for a small canopy, with the bands painted only in black;

Four *termes* (human figure supporting a column) in cross stitch;

The seven planets in *petit point* enriched with gold and silver;

The emblem of the star in cross stitch (*gros point*), not completed;

The North Star, not completed;

52 different flowers in *petit point* drawn from life, of which 32 are uncut, the rest cut each in its square;

124 birds of different kinds, in *petit point*, also drawn from life, uncut;

116 others, some cut;

16 four-footed beasts, also in *petit point*, including a lion attacking a boar, counted as one;

52 fish of different kinds;

The valance of a bed, prepared for a design of ovals;

Seven embroidered figures of women playing musical instruments;

Two ovals of the same size, to make a border;

Two tigers, and flower sprays, to apply to the above valance;

A floral square with dove-coloured ground, trimmed with carnation satin and fringe; and

Another square, cross stitch, with a peacock's tail, trimmed as above.

In addition there was a small square worked in braid stitch by the Countess of Lennox, the mother of Darnley, while she was kept in the Tower of London in 1574 – a rather surprising memento from the mother-in-law who held Mary responsible for the death of her son.

At the time the Chartley list was made, Mary had still one embroiderer, Charles Plouvart, working for her. He was dismissed as unnecessary with others of her staff, and was not among the faithful few allowed to remain until her execution. We may take it, therefore, that little, if any, new needle-work was begun after his departure. Apart from the teasing problem of what happened to these many embroideries after Mary's death, the inventory furnishes many clues as to her method of working. As has been suggested, her preference would probably be for small pieces that could be worked in the hand on a small frame or on a cushion covered with parchment on which work could be mounted. Indeed, in the final distribution two of these *tabourets* or sewing cushions were given to her apothecary together with 'All her confitures, succates, preserves, conserves and other medicinable drugges'.

The list shows that after nearly twenty years of imprisonment the Queen was still embroidering on silk and canvas – the greater part on canvas – to be made up into furnishings, mainly beds. Since her own needs were limited, many may have been intended as gifts: the gifts she showered so liberally on her ladies and others during her brief stay in Scotland. If this were so, however, it seems strange that no mention of such a gift was found in Mary's correspondence which has been sifted with such care by all those who have written about her.

Besides the bed at Scone Palace with the 'little flowers on canvas' applied to its crimson velvet which is thought to have been worked by Mary during her time in Scotland, part of a handsome bed, now at Parham Park, Sussex, is attributed to her and her ladies during her captivity in England. The bed is hung with curtains and valances of remarkable Hungarian point or 'flame stitch', which belong to the seventeenth century, but the back, canopy and bed cover are said to be the work of the Queen of Scots. They are embroidered on cream satin, with scrolling curves of gold thread enlivened with foliage and conventional flowers in coloured silks. The MA monogram and the fleur-de-lys give colour to the attribution. The bed came to Parham from Wroxton Abbey, Norfolk, whose owner at the time was Sir William Pope, grandson of Sir Thomas Pope, the founder of Trinity College, Oxford. Sir William was only thirteen at the time of the Queen's execution, and was created Earl of Downe by Charles I in 1628.

The bed, a regal piece of rich embroidery, would have required a large frame, and is not made up from the smaller pieces that have come to be associated with the Queen. It is a highly professional work, but there is no reason to suppose that the embroiderer employed by the Queen spent his time solely in drawing out designs for her and her ladies to work. He must on occasion have been asked to undertake work which he completed himself. On the other hand, although an embroiderer is mentioned once or twice during the queen's captivity in England, it is by no means certain that she had one on her staff continuously during these years, and in addition, because of the limited numbers of attendants that she was allowed, many members of her staff had to undertake duties other than those that their titles suggested. In particular a priest, although officially forbidden, could be introduced in another capacity. It is extremely difficult, therefore, to assess the amount of completed work produced from the queen's limited household during these years.

Until further evidence is uncovered, the beautiful bed at Parham must be admired for its own sake. The canopy and headboard, the coverlet and flame stitch curtains are all superlative examples of the art of needlework.

An unfinished piece, not mentioned in the Chartley inventory and which may therefore have been begun during the last months of the queen's life, is the 'furniture for a bed, of network and holland, not half finished'. This was left to Jane Kennedy. It was made of squares of *lacis* joined to rectangles of

linen. This type of embroidery was more common on the Continent than in
England, although an inventory taken at Worksop Manor in 1591, one of
Shrewsbury's houses, mentions 'a vallence of nett worke with whyt frynge',
and Mary had been a prisoner there for a brief period. A square of *lacis* was
exhibited in the Tercentenary Mary Queen of Scots Exhibition, Peterborough,
in 1887 (No. 116), said to have been worked by the Queen at Fotheringhay.
Nothing is known of its previous history, but it is expertly worked, and shows
a typical design of a hawk or falcon. Beds of network never became fashionable
in Britain, although netted canopies for four-poster beds can be found in the
United States dating from colonial times.

In the will made before James was born, Mary had been careful to indicate how her needlework was to be distributed. Before her execution, with little left except a few personal mementos, she must have been even more solicitous about the final bestowal of these last works of her needle: the emblems and *impresas* of those she had known, some of the innocent-seeming panels with barbed mottos, the still-unmounted birds, beasts and fishes made during her years at Sheffield. Jane Kennedy was given charge of distributing 'at her discretion' all the queen's linen: the 'eight payre of sheets, which served for the sayd Q. own bedd, 12 pillober[e]s, fyve dozen of smockes, dyvers hand-kerchers, some wrought, some playne', with the towels, bands and falls, coifs and veils, night rails and 'all her other pieces of common linen'. She would also have been told by Mary to whom each piece of needlework should be given. They are not detailed in the last list, and must therefore have been regarded as some of the 'other small things not mentioned in the Inventarye'. Rallay received all the 'Sowing silk and rawe silk of all colours'.

Inevitably, given the nearly nineteen years' imprisonment, during which her chief solace was embroidery, Mary is credited with many pieces which she may or may not have worked. The panels bearing her cipher or initials may be accepted as authentic. It is ingenuous to believe that all the pieces attributed to her were worked by her, just as it is unnecessarily sceptical to reject everything that is not signed. The signed pieces were not so marked in order to convince posterity. The cruciform panels with creatures taken from Gesner's *Icones Animalium* may have been initialled merely to prevent them from being quietly acquired by Bess of Hardwick. The cushion cover with the vine and the pruning hook, sent to Norfolk, bears the cipher from her signet ring. The panel bearing the arms of England, Scotland, France and Spain is not signed, but it bears unmistakable evidence of her workmanship, and may confidently be identified as the square mentioned in the Chartley inventory of 1586. Like the bed described by William Drummond, much of the output of these years has disappeared; some may still be preserved, its origin forgotten or hidden. We ought perhaps to be touched that, four hundred years after Mary chose the designs, selected the silks, and stitched the pieces bearing her monogram, we are still able to enjoy the liveliness and the subtlety of her skill.

12 The Oxburgh hangings

The embroideries that can most confidently be regarded as Mary's work are those bearing her crowned initials or cipher, that is, her initials MA superimposed on the Greek letter φ for the initial of her first husband, Francis II of France. This cipher was engraved on the hidden underside of her signet ring that bore the arms of Scotland. The cipher also appears on a little silver handbell that belonged to the Queen, on her book stamp, and also on a small cannon, believed to have been given to Sir Thomas Ker of Ferniehurst. It is fortunate that she chose to sign so many of her completed pieces: without this evidence the identification of her work would be much more difficult.

One such signed piece can be seen at Hardwick Hall, which now belongs to the National Trust and contains the richest collection of Elizabethan needlework in England. Mary did not, of course, ever visit Hardwick Hall: Bess had bought Hardwick, her family home and her birthplace, from her brother in 1570, and had built a handsome mansion around the modest manor house. When the Earl of Shrewsbury died in 1590 and Bess was widowed for the fourth time, she immediately began the building of a much more spacious and elegant house on the rising ground above her birthplace. This is the house that survives, one of the most beautiful of Elizabethan buildings. Many of the pieces of needlework there can be identified from the list of furnishings drawn up by Bess in 1601. Some were completed during the time that the Shrewsburys had custody of the Queen of Scots. Other pieces now preserved there could not have been made until the house was being built.

There are yards of the twisted renaissance cord design (Diagram 1) – the motif that is invariably read as the initials of Mary Stuart – similar to that at Scone Palace, but worked with more assurance. There are 'slips' – the little flowers worked in fine tent stitch or cross stitch on canvas for applying to bed hangings or cushions. These 'slips' were of course by no means exclusive to the Queen of Scots and Bess of Hardwick. They were to be found in many other houses in England and Scotland until the end of the seventeenth century, and many have survived.

There are, however, two pieces of what may have once been a long cushion at Hardwick that can confidently be regarded as Mary's work. The ground of yellow silk tent stitch is divided by a twisted cord design, highlighted with gold and silver braid stitch into compartments which enclose the Scottish thistle, the English rose and the white lily of France. Worked on finer canvas in tent stitch are six applied roundels, and the remains of two more, all illus-

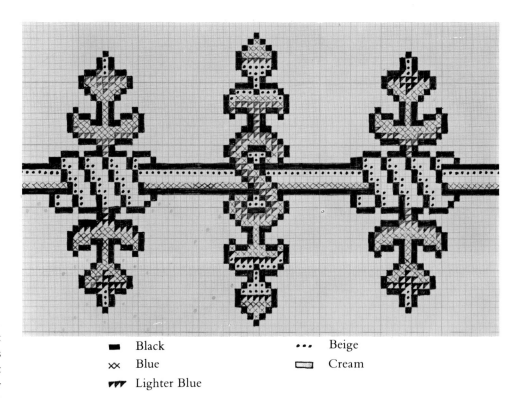

■ Black		••• Beige
✕✕ Blue		▭ Cream
▼▼▼ Lighter Blue		

*Diagram 1
Chart of renaissance twist design, worked in cross stitch, from a fragment at Hardwick Hall. (Dorothy M. Sim)*

trations of emblems, but without mottos. On one of these small roundels, showing two frogs on a well-head, there are the crowned initials ⋈R (Diagram 2). The cipher ⋈ was a common symbol for the name Mary: it was often used for the Virgin on church embroideries of the sixteenth and seventeenth centuries. But in this case the initials joined to the R for Regina, crowned, with the national flowers of Scotland, England and France, and especially the choice of emblems, all bear the stamp of the Queen of Scots. Four of the emblems have been identified by J. L. Nevinson as being copied from Gabriel Faerno's *Fables,* first published in Rome in 1563. The frogs on the well, debating whether to jump in or not, in case the well turns out to be dry, are symbolic of many situations during Mary's imprisonment, when she was tempted to fall in with dangerous plots in order to regain her freedom. The other emblems are equally apt, and have hidden meanings that could all be taken as reflections on her state of captivity, like the caged cat, surrounded by dancing mice, implying that the just are confined while the wicked go free.

Most of the pieces bearing Mary's initials or cipher can be seen at Oxburgh Hall, Norfolk, a beautiful moated manor-house of rosy brick with a soaring double-towered gatehouse which also belongs to the National Trust.

The hangings, embroidered panels mounted on green velvet, are displayed in the King's Room at Oxburgh Hall. One hangs over the fireplace, the others have been cut to make two curtains and a pelmet for an oak bed, carved with the initials A M I M and the date 1675. A fourth hanging, which was also at Oxburgh, had been cut up. Fragments of this hanging are in the Victoria and Albert Museum with some unmounted panels. Three other panels from the

*Opposite
Plate 51
Cushion cover with emblems in medallions (see plate 48). One, with frogs on a well, has the cipher of Mary in yellow silk. (The National Trust and the Victoria and Albert Museum, Crown Copyright.)*

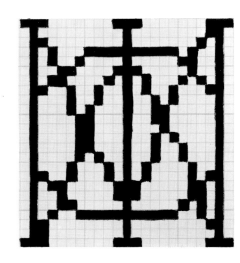

Left
Diagram 2
Chart of 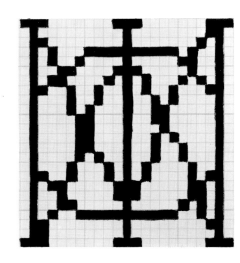 cipher on plate 51. (Dorothy M. Sim)

Right
Diagram 3
Chart of cipher on plate 84. (Dorothy M. Sim)

Plate 52
The King's Room,
Oxburgh Hall, Norfolk.
(The National Trust for
England and Wales.)

Plate 53
Panel PHESANT with
ⅯR cipher (see plate 65.)
(Victoria and Albert
Museum, Crown
Copyright, on loan to
Oxburgh Hall.)

Plate 54
Octagon. Monogram MARIE STVART crowned, with thistles, Mary's cipher, and motto SA VERTV MATIRE. (Victoria and Albert Museum, Crown Copyright, on loan to Oxburgh Hall.)

Plate 55
The Marian hanging, with
panels bearing Mary's cipher.
(Victoria and Albert
Museum, Crown Copyright,
on loan to Oxburgh Hall.)

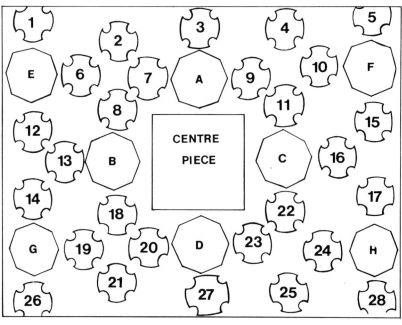

The Marian Hanging

Square centrepiece:

   The hand and the pruning hook   *(Plate 42)*

Octagons

A MARIE STVART with monogram   **(Plate 54)**
B PULCHIORI DETUR with apple tree   *(Plate 63)*
C ELIZABETH MARY (The bonds of virtue are
    straiter than that of blood   *(Plate 62)*
D GEORGE ELIZABETH SHREWSBURY E S
E Marigold turning to the sun   **(Plate 84)**
F Palm tree and tortoise   *(Plates 16 and 61)*
G LATET ANGUIS SUB HERBA (A snake lurketh in
    the grass)
H NE NIMIUM CREDE COLORI (Trust not
    overmuch in appearance)

Cruciform panels

1 SOLEN GOOSE on rocks
2 A JAY
3 PHENIX ⋈   **(Plate 35)**
4 TURTLE DOVE ⋈   *(Plate 86)*
5 DRAGON ℳℛ
6 A BYRD OF AMERICA ℳℛ   **(Plate 85)**
7 Eagle and hare with marigold and rose ℳℛ
8 AN VNICORNE ⋈   *(Plate 60)*
9 A PELLICAN ℳℛ
10 A COCKATRICE ⋈
11 A LYONE ⋈ crowned   *(Plate 58)*
12 A PHESANT ℳℛ   **(Plate 53)**
13 AN ONCE ⋈   *(Plate 64)*
14 ZYPHWHALE ℳℛ
15 BEES with beehive
16 A HARTE ℳℛ
17 SNEILES ⋈   *(Plate 80)*
18 A TIGER ⊗ crowned   *(Plate 87)*
19 DELPHINE ℳℛ crowned   **(Plate 37)**
20 A SEA MOONKE   *(Plate 30)*
21 A SCOLOPENDER
22 A HORSSE
23 A RHINOCEROTE OF THE SEA
24 BUTTERFLIES ℳℛ   *(Plate 66)*
25 A THORNE BACK
26 TROUTE, trout bridge and weir
27 (two panels joined vertically) A SHE DOLPHIN
    FISHE and another fish
28 THE CANKER, yellow rose and caterpillars ⋈   *(Plate 67)*

same hanging are at the Palace of Holyroodhouse, Edinburgh. Each of the original four hangings appears to have had a square centrepiece, surrounded by four octagonal panels and several cruciform panels of uniform size, embroidered in silks on canvas and applied to the green velvet which is further decorated with a scrolling trail of silver thread. Some of the panels bear Mary's initials or cipher, others the E S of Elizabeth Shrewsbury and some the monogram of George and Elizabeth Shrewsbury.

No hangings of this description can be found in the list made after the queen's execution. The Chartley inventory lists six pieces of tapestry of the history of Ravenna, six of the story of Meleager, two of the works of Hercules and three other pieces of 'a different sort'. We have seen in previous inventories that woven and embroidered hangings were apt to be lumped together. In this case the three 'of different sort' might possibly be construed as those now at Oxburgh, if it were not for the fact that in the final list made after Mary's execution at Fotheringhay, the six pieces of the history of Ravenna and the six of Meleager were all to be sold to pay the fares of her servants back home. In addition 'ten or twelve pieces of broken tapestrye', which must surely have comprised the rest of the hangings listed at Chartley, were left to one of her servants. Nevertheless even after this period of time the Oxburgh hangings could scarcely be described as 'broken', despite the fact that they appear to have been in constant use ever since they were brought there.

An overwhelming argument against their having been used as hangings, either on a bed or on the walls, by Mary at the end of her life is the presence of so many Shrewsbury and Cavendish initials. It seems improbable, to say the least, that she would wish to be reminded of her Shrewsbury jailers to the extent of having panels of Bess's embroidery mounted on hangings that she used herself.

However, the Chartley inventory contains a remarkable number of uncut or unmounted embroideries that are similar to those on the green velvet hangings. As well as the square bearing the arms of England, France, Spain and Scotland, there were 124 birds of various kinds, in *petit point* and drawn from life, uncut; 116 others, some cut; 16 four-footed beasts; and 52 kinds of fish. These would be more than ample for the birds, beasts and fishes that make the Oxburgh hangings such a source of lively interest to young and old today. They are described as worked in *petit point* which we now translate as tent stitch; the birds, beasts and fishes on the hangings are worked mainly in silk cross stitch, but we can by no means be sure that the names given to stitches in the sixteenth century are those by which we call them today.

Before her death Mary arranged for the bestowal of all her belongings: her needlework, listed so carefully the previous summer, must have also been allotted as very personal mementos for those for whom she felt affection. Her golden rosary, which she wore at her execution, and her prayer book were sent to Ann Dacre, wife of Philip Howard, then a prisoner in the Tower.

Among Mary's bequests at her death was the white veil which she wore to her execution. This was given to Ann, from whom it passed to the Society of Jesus, a house for whom she founded at Ghent. From the Jesuits it passed to Mary's descendant, the Cardinal of York. Together with these legacies it would seem probable that the square intended for Philip Howard, by now a prisoner in the Tower, would also have been sent to his wife, together with some of the unmounted birds and beasts, for Ann Dacre was a notable needlewoman. It is significant that among the birds, fishes and animals of the hanging most intimately connected with Mary, the square centrepiece is the same design as the fateful cushion sent to the Duke of Norfolk, Philip's father: the hand holding the pruning hook cutting down the unfruitful branches of the vine. Unless this is a duplicate – which would seem unlikely – the Howards would be the family most likely to possess it.

How, then, could the Shrewsbury and the Cavendish memorial panel and those initialled E S come to be included? Ann Dacre, Countess of Arundel (her husband was not allowed to use his father's title of Duke of Norfolk), lived till 1630. She bore Philip two children: a girl, who died in her teens, and Thomas, who was born after his father had entered the Tower. They were brought up very quietly by their mother. With the accession of James to the throne of England the family's fortunes were restored, although Ann still remained a staunch Catholic. Her son Thomas, Earl of Arundel, married a granddaughter of Bess of Hardwick – Alathea Talbot, daughter and heiress of Gilbert, seventh Earl of Shrewsbury (the son of Mary's custodian) and Mary Cavendish (Bess's youngest daughter).

It would seem probable that Alathea, finding this collection of unmounted embroideries which the Queen had sent to her mother-in-law, Ann Dacre, decided to have them mounted on green velvet and made into hangings, either for Arundel Castle or Arundel House in the Strand. Other panels of the same shape and size, made when Bess and Mary were on good terms, must have been lying at Sheffield Castle or Worksop Manor. Two have recently come to light at Hardwick, and the size and shape of the squares, octagons and cross-shaped pieces must have provided the inspiration for these green velvet hangings, adorned with the needlework of the Queen, of Bess and of any others who had added to the store of birds and beasts on canvas.

The Oxburgh panels are said to have been brought there from Cowdray Park in 1761, following the marriage of Sir Richard Bedingfeld, fourth Baronet, to Mary Browne, daughter of the sixth Viscount Montagu of Cowdray Park, Sussex. Though staunchly Catholic, the Bedingfeld family had no connection with Mary, and although Sir Anthony Browne, first Viscount Montagu (1528–92) was a Commissioner at Mary's trial at Fotheringhay and also a Catholic, he was fiercely loyal to Elizabeth who respected his honesty and visited him for a week at Cowdray in 1590.

It seems more likely that the panels went originally to Arundel and from there found their way to Cowdray. The Howard and the Montagu families were related, as the second wife of the first Viscount Montagu was Ann Dacre's aunt, and they were also Catholic at a time when priests were passed from one house to another to be hidden and avoid arrest.

The embroidered panels are mounted very professionally by an expert *tapissier*, each in its padded tailored frame of damask or brocade, some of it woven with gold thread. They are applied with great exactitude, and with a significance that may now elude us. The centrepiece of the hanging, now

Plate 56
The Cavendish hanging. A BYRDE OF AMERICA bears the M̃R monogram. (Victoria and Albert Museum, Crown Copyright, on loan to Oxburgh Hall.)

Plate 57
The Shrewsbury hanging. The Reindeer and Milkmaid panel bears the MR monogram.
(Victoria and Albert Museum, Crown Copyright, on loan to Oxburgh Hall.)

called the 'Marian' since it bears most of the panels displaying her initials, is the square with the hand wielding the pruning hook. It is framed in padded red damask outlined with a once yellow cord. The corners are held down by padded bosses of silk, two bearing a thistle, the other two a marigold. Above is an octagon with the letters of the name MARIA STVART superimposed with the queen's cipher, the royal crown, the thistle and the anagram motto 'Sa Virtu Matire'. Above this is a cruciform panel of the 'phenix', not tiré au naturel (taken from life) from a book of natural history such as Gesner or Belon, but shown in heraldic fashion rising from the flames; the impresa of Mary's mother, Marie de Guise. Beside the upper corners of the central square are two animals, the 'lyone' and 'unicorne', placed as in the royal arms of Scotland: the unicorn on the left, not the right as in the English royal arms. The rest of the hangings have at some time been cut up and altered, so that the significance of the arrangement may well be lost.

Some thirty panels bear the queen's cipher or monogram. The most unmistakable is the octagon above the pruning-hook square. The queen's cipher (Diagram 3) is even more distinct on the emblem of the marigold turning towards the sun, with its Latin motto 'Non Inferiora Secutus' ('Not following lower things') which Mary had taken as her own. Another octagon shows the crowned palm tree with a land tortoise climbing the stem with the motto 'Dat Gloria Vires' ('Glory gives strength'): the design of the silver ryal (Plate 15) ordered in 1565 to replace the one in which Darnley's name had taken precedence over her own. An even less explicable octagon contains the letters of the names ELIZABETH MARY superimposed under a royal crown flanked by the thistle, marigold and another unidentifiable flower, with the motto 'Virtutis Vincula Sanguinis Arctiora' ('The bonds of virtue are straiter than those of blood'). It may possibly refer to Queen Elizabeth – as could the opposite octagon, which shows an apple tree with the barbed motto 'Pulchriori Detur' ('Be it given to the fairer').

The smaller cruciform panels signed by the Queen are those that most tease our curiosity. We can understand her choice of the leaping dolphin, with its pun on the title of Dauphin, just as we can understand the 'lyone', that king of beasts, and the tiger, set like the Holyrood 'catte' and the 'once' (ounce) on a chequered floor. The pheasant, copied from Gesner's elegant woodcut, was not excluded because it would not fit within the uniform limits of the canvas: instead, the remainder of its long tail was laid neatly above its body. The despair in the yellow rose eaten by 'canker' is understandable, and the 'butterflies' with MR in red may suggest her faith, for the butterfly was the symbol of the soul and immortality.

Not all the creatures were chosen for their symbolic meaning. The 'falconet', the 'kestrel', the 'hobreau' (hobby falcon), although unsigned, were surely chosen by someone who loved, as she did, hawking and falconry. Yet even here there may be a hidden meaning, for 'hobreau' as well as being the bird that could be trained to retrieve game also meant, as Cotgrave reminds us, someone of mean birth, who aspired to be higher than he was. Could the choice have been made by one who spoke French and with Bess in mind? And the equally anonymous 'gleade' (the kite), with a frog regarding it with beady eye, may have recalled the satirical Scottish poem of 1567: 'Ane gled aye gaipand guid men to devour'.

The 'byrde of America', the toucan with its unmistakable beak, bears the queen's monogram, and seems an unlikely choice. However, the toucan is native to Brazil, which was discovered by a Frenchman, Jean Cousin. Later, Jean de Lèry, the Calvinist pastor who accompanied the abortive expedition to Rio de Janeiro in 1555, wrote an account describing how the natives decked themselves out in feathers, including those of the ostrich and toucan. Among the queen's belongings left behind in Edinburgh were small curiosities brought with her from France, such as 'Ane paper of fedderis [feathers] of all sorts', and 'The Beik of a fowle of India or Brazile'.

The unsigned 'beaver' with blue tail and eddying waves reminds us that, although these animals were by then rare if not extinct in France and Britain, Jacques Cartier, who had annexed Newfoundland and Canada to France in 1534, described the profusion of beaver he had seen in his exploration of the St. Lawrence.

The other 'byrd of America', which is also signed by the Queen, is not so easily explained as the toucan. In shape it is very close to the *'Pic verd Jaulne'* illustrated by Belon. The silk of the bird's embroidery has worn in parts, but one can still see that it is yellow with a brown tail and spots, and that it bears a striking resemblance to the yellow-shafted flicker *(Colaptes auratus)* of the eastern seaboard of North America.

Finally the panel signed MR and labelled 'Jupiter', is almost certainly a dog *tiré au naturel* (drawn from life), one of the pet dogs that Mary kept around her until the last instant of her life.

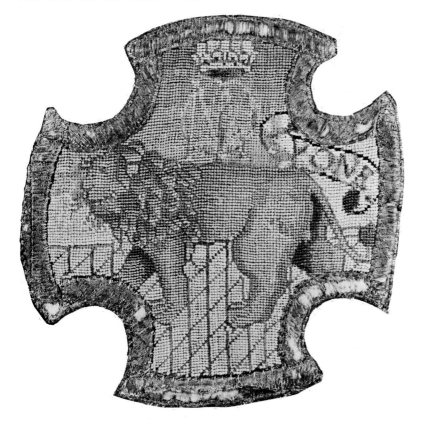

Above
Plate 59
The Lion. C. Gesner *Icones Animalium* 1560. (The University of Edinburgh.)

Left

Plate 58
Panel. LYONE with Mary's cipher. (Victoria and Albert Museum, Crown Copyright, on loan to Oxburgh Hall.)

Plate 60
Panel. AN UNICORNE
with Mary's cipher. (Victoria
and Albert Museum, Crown
Copyright, on loan to
Oxburgh Hall.)

Plate 61
Octagon. Palm Tree and
Tortoise (see plate 16).
(Victoria and Albert
Museum, Crown Copyright,
on loan to Oxburgh Hall.)

Plate 62
Octagon. ELIZABETH
MARY. (Victoria and Albert
Museum, Crown Copyright,
on loan to Oxburgh Hall.)

Plate 63
Octagon. *'Pulchriori Detur'*
('Be it given to the fairest').
(Victoria and Albert
Museum, Crown Copyright,
on loan to Oxburgh Hall.)

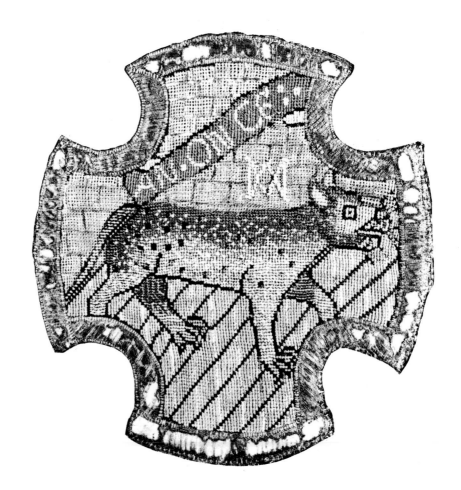

Plate 64
Panel. ONCE with ⋈
cipher. (Victoria and Albert
Museum, Crown Copyright,
on loan to Oxburgh Hall.)

Plate 65
Pheasant. C. Gesner *Icones
Animalium* 1560. (The
University of Edinburgh.)

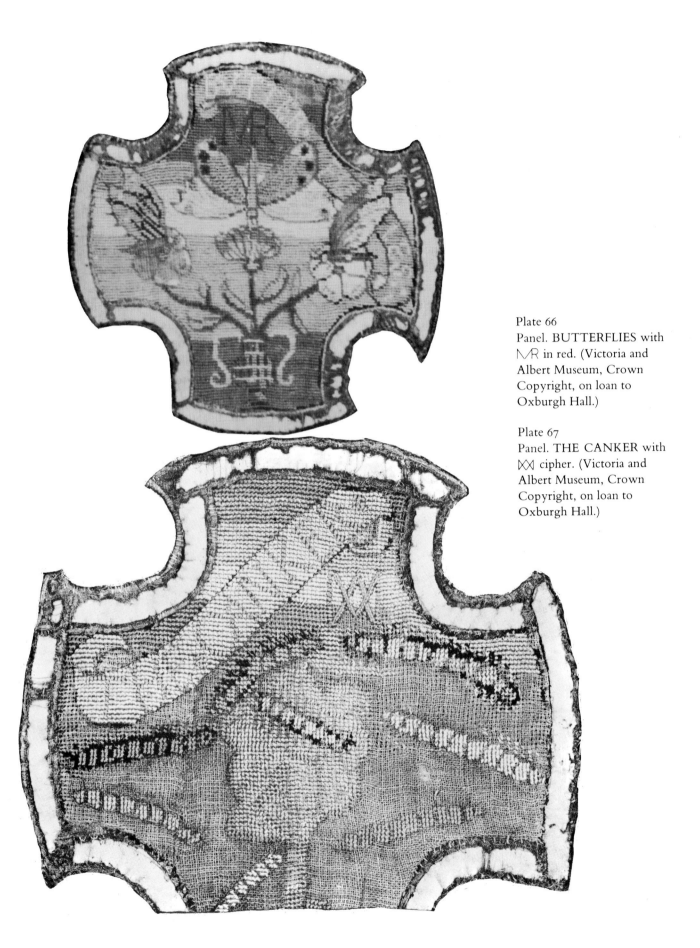

Plate 66
Panel. BUTTERFLIES with ΛΛR in red. (Victoria and Albert Museum, Crown Copyright, on loan to Oxburgh Hall.)

Plate 67
Panel. THE CANKER with ⋈ cipher. (Victoria and Albert Museum, Crown Copyright, on loan to Oxburgh Hall.)

Plate 68
GLEADE on the 'Cavendish'
hanging. (Victoria and
Albert Museum, Crown
Copyright, on loan to
Oxburgh Hall.)

Plate 69
The Toucan. C. Gesner
Icones Animalium 1560. (The
University of Edinburgh.)

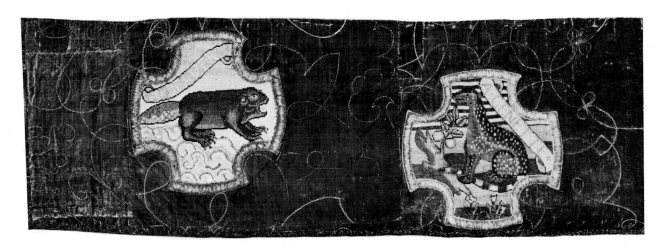

Plate 70
Portion of valance. Beaver
and Genette. (Victoria and
Albert Museum, Crown
Copyright, on loan to
Oxburgh Hall.)

Plate 71
The Beaver. C. Gesner
Icones Animalium 1560. (The
University of Edinburgh.)

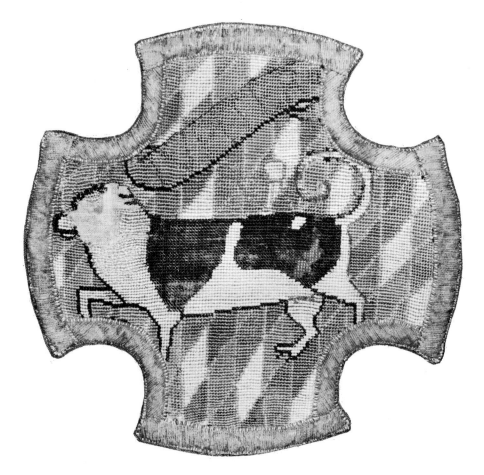

Plate 72
JUPITER with ΛR
monogram. (Victoria and
Albert Museum, Crown
Copyright, on loan to
Oxburgh Hall.)

Plate 73
Elephant. C. Gesner *Icones Animalium* 1560. (The University of Edinburgh.)

Plate 74
Panel. ELEPHANT. (Victoria and Albert Museum, Crown Copyright, on loan to Oxburgh Hall.)

Plate 75
A BOATE FISHE. (Victoria and Albert Museum,
Crown Copyright, on loan to Oxburgh Hall.)

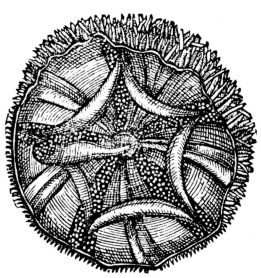

Plate 76
Echinops. C. Gesner *Icones Animalium* 1560. (The
University of Edinburgh.)

Plate 77
Reindeer and Milkmaid. C. Gesner *Icones Animalium*
1560. (The University of Edinburgh.)

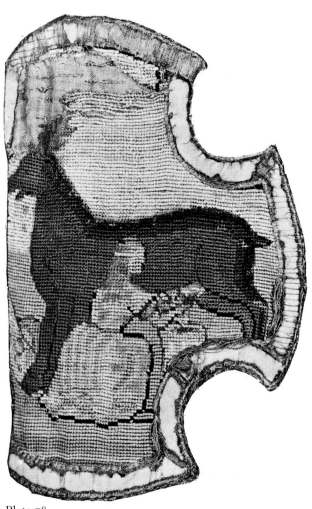

Plate 78
Reindeer and Milkmaid with ᴍR on Shrewsbury
Hanging. (Victoria and Albert Museum, Crown
Copyright, on loan to Oxburgh Hall.) 115

Plate 79
Snails. C. Gesner *Icones Animalium* 1560. (The University of Edinburgh.)

Plate 81
Monkey. C. Gesner *Icones Animalium* 1560. (The University of Edinburgh.)

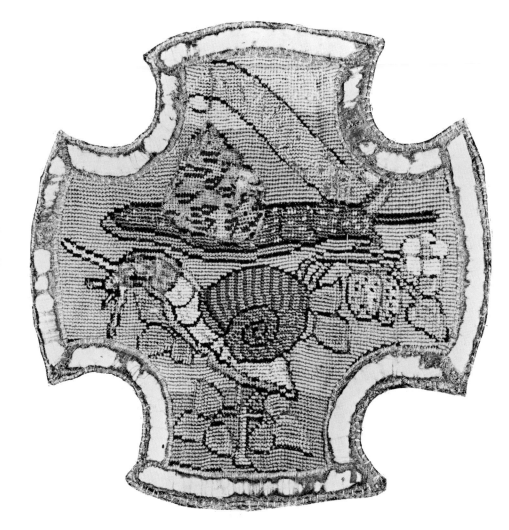

Plate 80
SNEILES with ⋈ cipher. (Victoria and Albert Museum, Crown Copyright, on loan to Oxburgh Hall.)

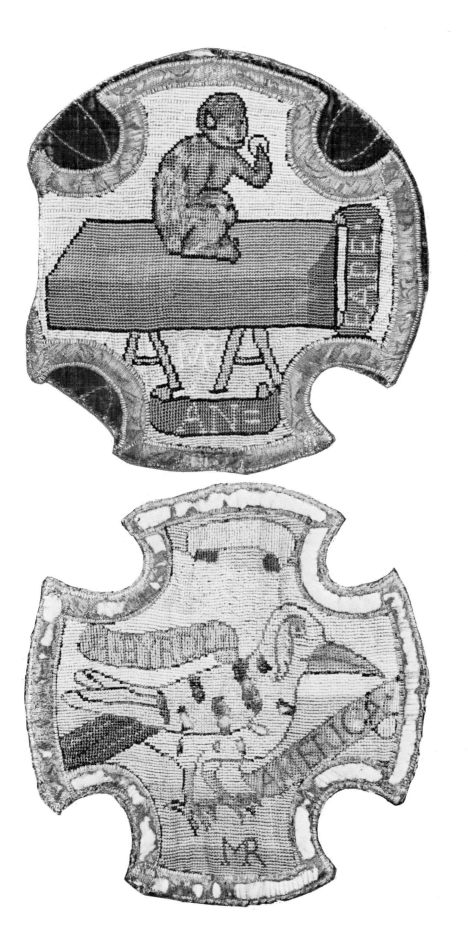

Plate 82
AN EAPE with ⋀R monogram. (Victoria and Albert Museum, Crown Copyright, on loan to Oxburgh Hall.)

Plate 83
A BYRDE OF AMERICA on the Cavendish Hanging with ⋀R. (Victoria and Albert Museum, Crown Copyright, on loan to Oxburgh Hall.)

Plate 84
Octagon. Marigold turning to the sun, with motto *'Non Inferiora Secutus'* **('not following lower things') and Mary's cipher.**

Opposite
Plate 85
A BYRD OF AMERICA (Toucan) with ᴍꞧ**. (See plate 69.) (Victoria and Albert Museum, Crown Copyright, on loan to Oxburgh Hall.)**

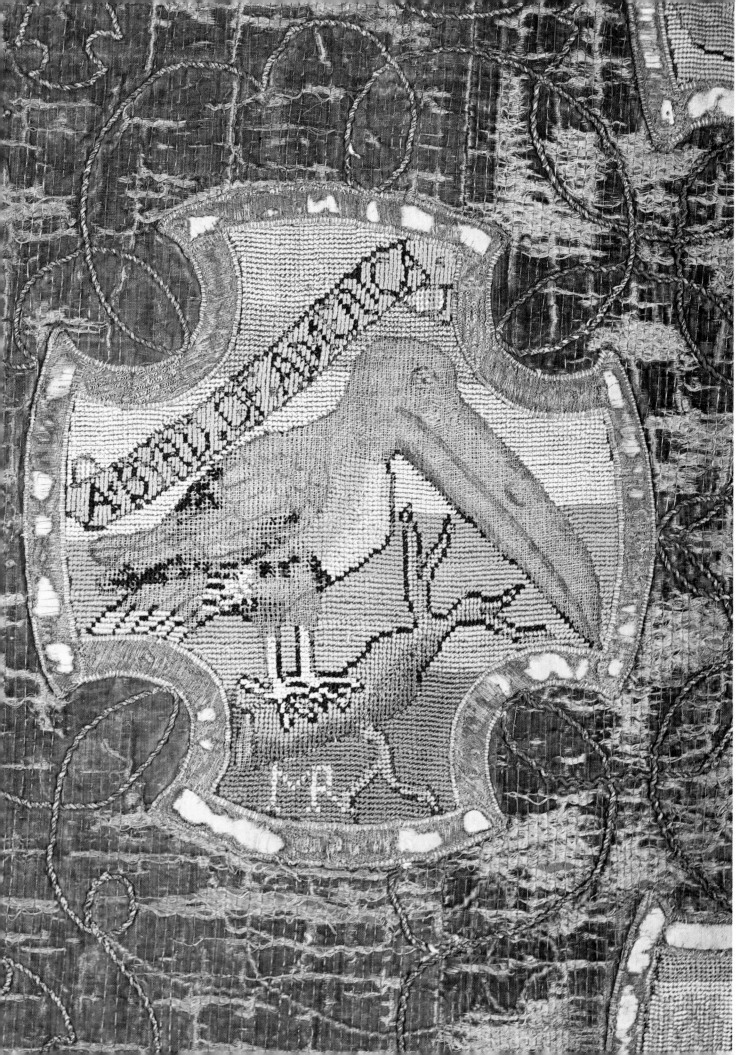

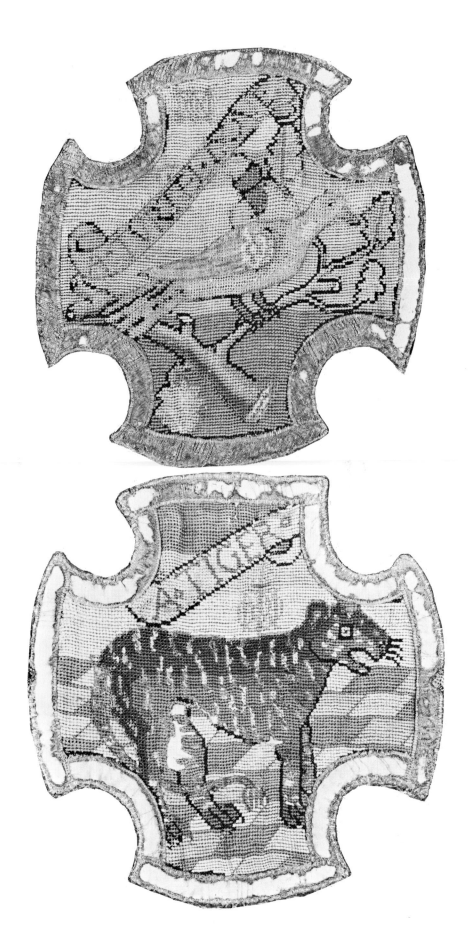

Plate 86
Panel. A TURTLE DOVE.

Plate 87
Panel. A TIGER.

13 Envoi

The needlework listed in 1586 at Chartley and the pieces now remaining allow us to guess at Mary's taste and skill as a needlewoman. In her childhood she had learnt to embroider – like all girls of her generation and upbringing – as a necessary part of her education. Even during the most strenuous part of her life in Scotland, she did not consider it incongruous for a monarch to sew while she received ambassadors or listened to her advisers. It is, however, surprising that one so energetic and impetuous as Mary found pleasure in so quiet and meticulous a craft. During the nineteen years of her captivity, it became both a solace and a pastime. The 'devising of works' served not only to occupy her fingers and to fill the long empty days, but the design could have a double meaning, or an emblem with a tart motto, which would exercise her wit and help to assuage her burning sense of injustice.

She did not embroider for the sake of the stitches. The pieces that remain are not smoothly finished meticulous stitchery. They were drawn out for her with the shapes outlined in black silk. She filled in the colours with cross or tent stitch, shading as necessary from the silks available, enlivening the design with occasional chain or braid stitch to emphasise the lettering or to highlight the lozenge compartments of the cushions now at Hardwick. She used a singularly limited range of stitches, and does not appear to have shared the contemporary passion of English needlewomen for intricate composite stitchery for its own sake, as catalogued by John Taylor the Water Poet, in *The Needle's Excellency* (tenth edition, 1634).

Although we know that she was capable of '. . . Tente worke, Raised worke, Laide worke . . . Net worke . . .' she does not appear to have been attracted by the complicated performance of the coiled stems, of plaited braid stitch or what is now called Ceylon stitch or the detached buttonhole filling, that riot of technique that was to lead to the raised-work pictures and boxes of the following century.

She had been educated in France, and to the end of her days she remained a Frenchwoman, sufficiently French for every piece she planned to be functional, able to be used as the need arose for some article of dress or furnishing, for a cushion or a valance or to be applied to a bed or wall hanging.

For Mary Stuart the design was always more important than the technique. Even on the skirt for Queen Elizabeth, if – as seems possible – it is indeed her work, the stitches are subordinate to the design of the pink, rose, lily and thistle in a controlled framework of silver scrolls.

In all the pieces that remain, although the silks are worn and the colours muted by the centuries, although the drawing is that of her embroiderer, the design, the colour and the stitchery reflect an urgent lively intelligence, condemned to translate into small panels of needlework the memories, aspirations and bitterness of a stormy, unhappy and tragic Queen.

Plate 88
Child's Reins, said to have been embroidered by
Mary Queen of Scots for her son, James VI. Arundel
Castle. (The Duke of Norfolk.)

Plate 89
Child's Reins. Detail of breastplate. Pink silk
embroidered with metal thread.

Diagram 4
Blackwork design from the
Earl of Moray's shirt, plate 15.
(Agnes M. Leach)

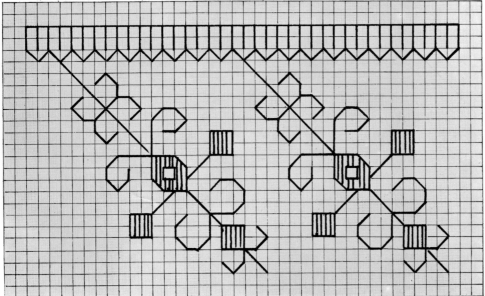

Diagram 5
Chart of design from the
Earl of Moray's shirt. (Agnes
M. Leach)

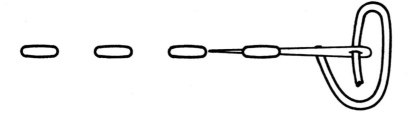

Diagram 6
Double-running or Holbein
stitch, used in Blackwork.

Diagram 7
Method of darning net in
lacis:
a – b straight darning
c – d diagonal darning
(Agnes M. Leach)

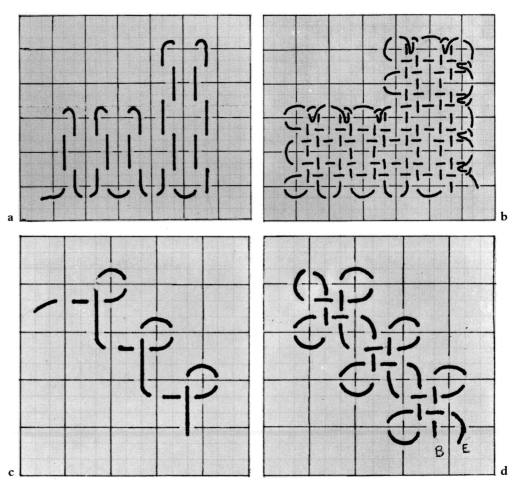

Diagram 8
Chart of the crowned heart.
(Agnes M. Leach)

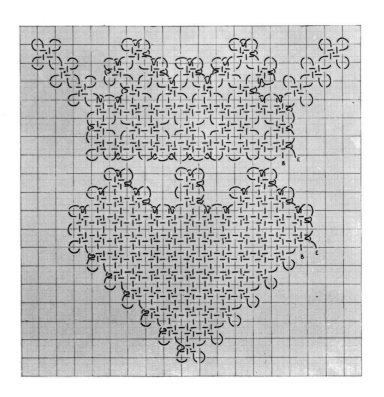

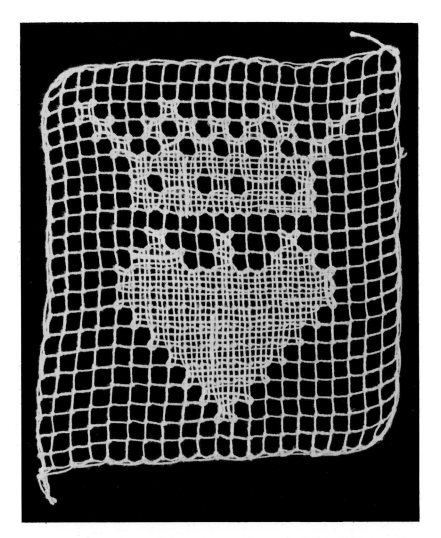

Diagram 9a
Lacis motif: crowned heart.
(Agnes M. Leach)

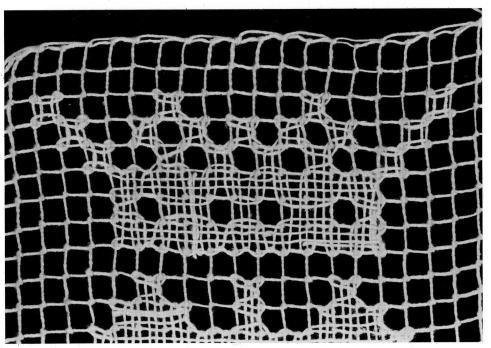

Diagram 9b
Detail. (Agnes M. Leach)

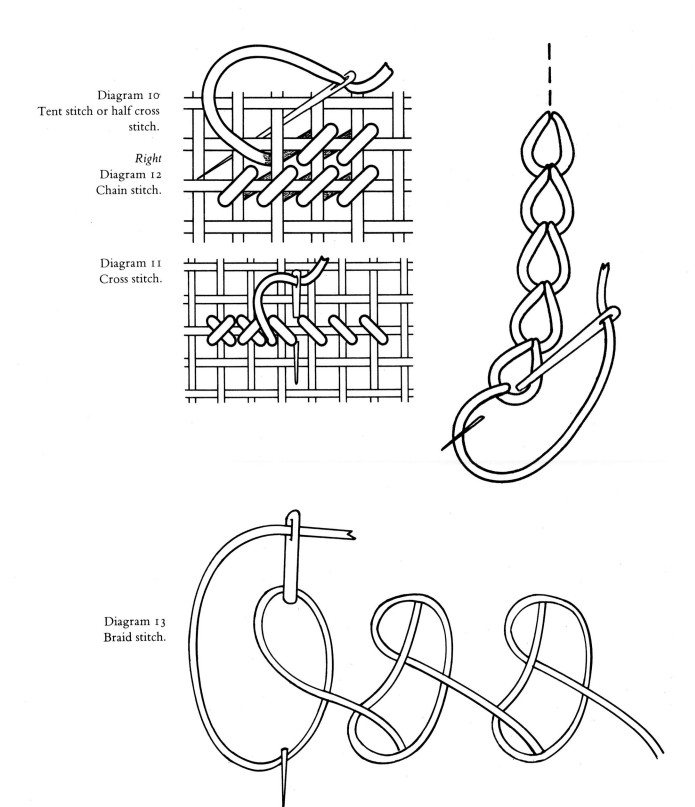

Diagram 10
Tent stitch or half cross stitch.

Right
Diagram 12
Chain stitch.

Diagram 11
Cross stitch.

Diagram 13
Braid stitch.

Further Reading

France

Farcy, Louis de: *La Broderie du XIe siècle jusqu'à nos jours*, two volumes (Paris, 1890)

Fraser, Antonia: *Mary, Queen of Scots* (London, 1969)

Freeman, Rosemary: *English Emblem Books* (London, 1948)

Labanoff, Prince A.: *Lettres et mémoires de Marie, Reine d'Écosse*, seven volumes (Paris, 1844)

Lotz, Arthur: *Bibliographie der Modelbücher* (Stuttgart, 1963)

Vasselot, Jean-Joseph Marguet de: *Bibliographie de la tapisserie, de tapis et de la broderie en France* (Paris, 1935)

Ruble, Alphonse de: *La première jeunesse de Marie Stuart* (Paris, 1891)

Cotgrave, Randle: *Dictionarie* for translation of contemporary French terms (London, 1611)

Wardle, Patricia: The Embroideries of Mary Queen of Scots: Notes on the French Background *Bulletin of the Needle and Bobbin Club* (New York, Vol. 64, Nos. 1 & 2, 1981, pp. 3–14)

Scotland

Fleming, D. H.: *Mary, Queen of Scots* (London, 1897)

Labanoff, Prince A.: *Lettres et mémoires de Marie, Reine d'Écosse*, Volume II (Paris, 1844)

McGeorge, A.: *Illustrations of the reign of Mary, Queen of Scots* (Maitland Club, Glasgow 1834. Papers from the Scots College, Paris)

Robertson, J.: *Inventaires de la Royne Descosse, 1556–1569* (Bannatyne Club Edinburgh No. 111, 1863)

Swain, M. H.: *Historical needlework, a study of influences in Scotland and Northern England* (London, 1970)

Swain, M. H.: *The Lochleven and Linlithgow Hangings in Proceedings of the Society of Antiquaries of Scotland* Vol.124, (1994) pp.455–466.

Thomson, T.: *Collection of inventories and other records of the royal wardrobe* (Edinburgh, 1815)

England

Digby, G. Wingfield: *Elizabethan embroidery* (London, 1963)

Labanoff, Prince A.: *Lettres et mémoires de Marie, Reine d'Écosse*, Volume VII (Paris, 1844)

Leader, J. D.: *Mary, Queen of Scots, in captivity* (London, 1880)

Nevinson, J. L.: *Catalogue of English domestic embroidery* (London, 1950)

Nevinson, J. L.: *English domestic embroidery patterns of the sixteenth and seventeenth century* (Walpole Society XXVIII, 1939–40)

Norfolk, Duke of (edited by): *The lives of Philip Howard and of Anne Dacres, his wife* (London, 1857)

Williams, E. Carleton: *Bess of Hardwick* (London, 1959)

Williams, Neville: *Elizabeth I, Queen of England* (London, 1967)

Williams, Neville: *Thomas Howard, Duke of Norfolk* (London, 1963)

Zulueta, F. de: *Embroideries by Mary Stuart and Elizabeth Talbot at Oxburgh Hall, Norfolk* (Oxford, 1923)

Index